Daniel and The Visions
about the End Time

By
Toby Joreteg

Aspect Books
Brushton, New York 12916

Published by

Aspect Books
P.O. Box 542
Brushton, New York 12916

Dedication

To My Friend and Savior Jesus Christ

Contents

Preface

The book of Daniel is a fascinating book. Many have tried to understand the context in these chapters. Up till the end of Chapter 11, there has been some kind of agreement in the understanding of the prophecy. From there until the very end of this book, the most different aspects and interpretations can be found. You may wonder why? Since we know that some prophecies have been sealed to the time of the end, it seems the more interesting to dig into the Scripture to read and study and ask the Holy Spirit for guidance and revelation. Everyone with Christian background is realizing that this world is about to come to an end, and if that is the case, God will also be willing to take away the seal of this prophecy, to give spiritual food to His believers at the right time. God stands to His word and is waiting for us to ask for understanding. In several of the prophecies in the Book of Daniel, it took some time before God revealed the interpretation. That was the case for the unsealed parts of the prophecy. When it comes to the sealed parts of the prophecy, it is even more exciting. Is it time for this revelation today? As a Christian we should always be alert and ready for the next step of God. But at some point, the time is fulfilled, and maybe today is the day of God's revelation of the unsealed parts in the Book of Daniel.

Introduction

When reading and studying prophetic books in the Bible, it is very important to understand the situation when it occurred. It is true that we always shall try to apply what we find in the Scripture to see what we can learn from it today. But still, the real meaning of the prophecy must be found in the circumstances when it was given. What was happening at that time? What was the need and the perspective? What was the background? Who is the prophecy aimed at, etc.? And there should be a lot of questions like that. But when we do this, it makes sense from academic and logical perspective. Is that enough? Absolutely not. If you think and act as if the Bible is a science, you will never reach the goal. You will end up with a logical explanation, which might impress some, but still be without the real truth. In John Chapter 4:23 we read that "the true worshipers will worship the Father in Spirit and Truth." That is the same as to say the Holy Spirit and Jesus Christ, since Jesus Himself tells us that He is the truth.

What I am trying to say is that your education can be to your advantage and to your disadvantage. Your lack of theological education can be to your advantage or your disadvantage. It all depends on your openness to God. God could use Paul, with one of the highest levels of education in those days. God could also use Peter as a disciple, without any education. What do they have in common? In Proverb Chapter 3:5, we read:

> *"Trust in the LORD of all your heart and lean not on your own understanding."*

This text is the basis for this book. The author has no theological training, no pastoral background, took very little time for God until recently. But some years back, everything changed. God touched my life in a very special way, and the trust relationship to God has been number one on the agenda. If you believe that God can come into someone's life and make a difference, you know what I am saying. If we are in touch with the Most High, as

Daniel often writes, no project can be too big, no under-standing too far to grasp, no word without God's interven-tion and explanation. Right now, you are encouraged to go on your knees and pray to God. Ask for His wisdom, un-derstanding and clarity of mind. If you can do that with all your heart, you have one thing in common with Paul and Peter, mentioned above. They were willing to sit down and be totally open for God. They were ready to trust Him and accept whatever He wanted to say. Think about Paul for a second. He had a lot to relearn. But, he was willing to 100%. He wanted the Spirit and the Truth to guide him. What about you?

If we look carefully into all 6 visions, we will find some differences, and several similarities. When studying this book of Daniel, there are three models that strike us. ①One type of prophecies is dealing with the world order in itself.②Another type of vision is dealing with the people of Daniel, the Israelites.③And then there is one vision dealing with the whole concept of prophecy. It is very important to distinguish these three components. Otherwise, we might end up at the wrong place. This is the reason for the studying order of the chapters in the book of Daniel as you will find them in this book. If we go from Daniel Chapter 1 and all the way to the end of Chapter 12, we might make mistakes, especially if we have preconceived ideas.

Vision 1…

Here we find a type of prophecy dealing with the world order. It is written down in Chapter 2. Here God is presenting the flow of the kingdoms in the world until the very end of this world. We find that the original vision was not seen by Daniel. It was seen by the great King Nebuchadnezzar. The King had forgotten his dream and asked all the wise men in his kingdom to tell him his dream and the interpretation. They all answered, "tell us the dream o king and then we will give you the interpretation." The king did not remember his dream and threatened their lives if they resisted or couldn't tell him the dream. The dream was later on revealed to Daniel, as well as the interpretation. With this, God was honored in a tremendous way. And Daniel, who gave all honor to God and God alone, was given high position. This is the background to all Daniel's visions and this should always be our background for all our actions. God and God alone is to be given glory.

The dream was unique in many ways. The time span goes from the Babylonian kingdom all the way till the second coming of Jesus Christ. This we can read in Daniel 2:44–45:

> *"In the time of those kings, the* **God of heaven will set up a kingdom** *that will never be destroyed, nor will it be left to other people. It will crush all those kingdoms and bring them to an end, but it will itself* **endure for ever**. *This is the meaning of the vision of the rock cut out of a mountain, but not by human hands…"*

So this is the great vision. It covers all the world's history to the second coming of Jesus. This vision is the backbone for all the other visions.

VISION 2…

This vision is about our understanding of prophecy. It is not dealing with the Israelites. This vision is not prophecy about the world order either but dealing especially with our thinking about prophecy. If God has determined everything before it happens, what is then our part? However, the dream has some very wide implications when it comes to the understanding of it. It is dealing with our attitude towards God and the prophecy coming from God. What is arranged by God, and what is our free will in this? It is a dream coming to Nebuchadnezzar about the enormous tree in Chapter 4. Of course, this dream was also dealing with the personal problems of the king.

VISION 3…

Starts in Chapter 7. Daniel was given both the vision and the interpretation. It also covers the world's history from that age all the way up till verse 11, where the beast is finally slain and thrown in the blazing fire. In verse 13 we read:

> *"In my vision at night I looked, and there before me was one like* **a son of man, coming with the clouds of heaven…"***

and in verse 27, the last part, it says that:

*"the kingdoms will be handed to the saints, the people of the Most High. **His kingdom will be an everlasting kingdom**, and all rulers will worship and obey Him."*

So again we see the whole world scenario to the end of age, with the second coming of Jesus as a climax. But why two visions about the same thing? Is there any difference?

VISION 4...

This is a vision of Daniel and we read it in Chapter 8 of Daniel. It starts with the current kingdom and in verse 19 it mentions the final scenario

*"He said: 'I am going to tell you what will happen later in the **time of the wrath**, because the vision concerns the appointed **time of the end.'"**

So for a second time, all world history in a flash? No, this vision is very special. This one can only be understood when we have built a solid foundation from visions 1 to 3 and especially from visions 5 to 6. Vision 4 is a masterpiece of prophecy. The time of the end and the time of wrath can only be understood in the right perspective. When it was given it was sealed for the future. Today it might be open for you. Your understanding of this prophecy depends only on you and your relationship to the Holy Spirit and Jesus Christ. With fixed paradigm, you will not see. With an open mind as Saul, you will enjoy.

VISION 5...

We can read in Chapter 9. It starts with the background of the Israelites. It tells us about their captivity in Babylon, and how long they have been there. In Daniel's prayer we also know why the Israelites are in Babylon, etc. Then in verse 24 it is spelled out in a very clear way:

*"Seventy 'sevens' are decreed **for your people** and*

> **your holy city** *to finish transgression, to put an end to sin, to atone for wickedness, to bring in everlasting righteousness, to seal up vision and prophecy and to anoint the most holy."*

"Your people" is, of course, the Israelites and their holy city is Jerusalem. From this people, the most holy one will also be anointed, which is the same as the anointing of Jesus, their Messiah. In the first visions, the Israelites are not specifically mentioned. In this vision five, we will find a lot of interesting things about the Israelites. The end of this vision is the end of sacrifice and offering, as we will see in verse 27. This is pointing to the death of Jesus Christ on the cross. Once, and for all, He died for us. But when does the prophecy really end? Does it end in AD 70 or AD 34?

Vision 6...

Starts in Chapter 10 and goes all the way to the end of the Book of Daniel in Chapter 12. In Daniel 10:14, the angel explains the purpose of the vision:

> *"Now I have come to explain to you what will happen to your people in the future, for the vision concerns a time yet to come."*

"Your people," here again is meant the people of Daniel, which are the Israelites. It talks about a time yet to come. It does not say the end time or the second coming of Jesus. It talks about a specific time, which we will study in detail later on. Yes, in Chapter 12, verse 4, we know that the knowledge to this vision will be sealed until the time of the end, but it does not say that the vision is about the end time. The last two visions seem to be addressed to the people of Daniel, the Israelites, and start with their historical situation in which Daniel lived and reach to the end of Israel as a chosen nation of God at AD 34. This last vision, in Chapters 10–12, is one of the least understood visions in the book of Daniel. Are you willing to go right into the exciting prophecy of Chapter 12? If so, buckle up, and here we go!

Daniel: Chapter 12

I can understand that you do not feel comfortable or used to understanding a Bible book by reading the last chapter first. But I can assure you that you can read about any vision in any order, and eventually you will get the message and the understanding you need. And later on you can link the chapters together. However, if the book has passages which are hard to understand, you have to approach a book in a different way. Another reason for this is that we are loaded with prejudice, both good and bad. To get a fresh start, it is better to focus on Chapter 12 first, since there are quite a few very strong and precise statements in this chapter. If we take these statements as they are, we must find good understanding and agreement with the rest of Daniel. If not, it is not worth reading. But if there is harmony between Chapter 12 and the other chapters in Daniel, it is a strong support for the following interpretation. Let us look at some of these specific passages.

MICHAEL AND THE BIG DISTRESS...

Let us start with verse 1 of Daniel, Chapter 12. But before we go on, we have to leave the first sentence for a little while and come back to it later.

> "At that time **Michael**, the great prince who protects your people, **will arise**. There will be a **time of distress such as has not happened** from the beginning of nations until then. But at that time your people—everyone whose name is found written in the book—will be delivered."

"At that time" is actually a very important time statement for the understanding of this chapter. On the other hand, if we decide upon a wrong historical time at this moment in our study, we will be trapped during the rest of the chapter. So let us leave this phrase for a while and see if there is something else that is convincing about the time period we are dealing with. The next thing mentioned is the "time of distress." Daniel is talking about a time of distress and saying that this is the worst one so far in history. There has been nothing like this in the past. The distress is so immense that nothing is comparable to this in all nations and during all times. Think about all events that have taken place so far in the world's history. Not even the judgment of the earth through the flood comes close in comparison. Think about all the wars on earth up till now. Those wars have caused a lot of distress for many people and nations, but this is more. It also says that Michael will arise. Could he be a part of the action or is he the solution? Who is this Michael? In Daniel 10:13 we read:

> *"But the prince of the Persian kingdom resisted me twenty-one days. Then **Michael**, one of the **chief princes**, came to help me, because I was detained there with the King of Persia."*

It seems to be that Gabriel was the one representing "I" in this verse. You can find that if you read Daniel 9:21. Gabriel is the one giving wisdom and understanding to Daniel as a messenger from God. What the above text is saying is: When the problem was too big for Gabriel, one of the chief princes stood up to help him. The name of that help is Michael. The problem seems not to be too big for Michael. He is mighty. In verse 20 and 21 of the same Chapter 10 in Daniel, we read another event where Michael was involved:

> *"So he said, 'Do you know why I have come to you? Soon I will return to fight against the prince of Persia, and when I go, the prince of Greece will come; but first I will tell you what is written in*

*the Book of Truth. (**No one supports me against them except Michael**, your prince...)'"*

This seems to be the same story as above. There is only one with power enough, and that is Michael. However, Michael the chief prince is not explained here either. We only know here about his powerful actions. In the Book of Daniel we cannot easily realize who Michael is; we need to go to other parts of the Bible. There are two things we need to solve to approach the understanding of Daniel 12:1. The first one is who Michael is and the second question is if we can find any correlation to an explicit time of distress. Let us look at Revelation Chapter 12 and verses 7–9:

*"And there was **war** in heaven. **Michael** and his angels fought against the dragon, and the dragon and his angels fought back. But he (the devil) was not strong enough, and they lost their place in heaven. **The great dragon was hurled down**—the ancient serpent called the devil, or **Satan**, who leads the whole world astray. He was hurled **to the earth**, and his angels with him."*

Here we find Michael again in a very important situation. He seems to be the number one fighting against the devil. Michael is so powerful that he wins the battle. However, have you noticed that the text talks about a war going on? As far as we can tell, there must have been a huge number of angels involved. If one third of them fight against two thirds of them, the battle must be immense. It is not a war with guns, but still it may be a war with a lot of stress. Maybe the outcome of this situation is of such immense proportions. Could this be the event with the big distress also? What kind of battle are we talking about? Let us continue to read Revelation 12:10–12:

*"Then I heard a loud voice in heaven say: '**Now** have come the **salvation** and the power and the **kingdom of our God**, and the authority of his **Christ**. For the accuser of our brothers, who accuses them before our God day and night, has been*

hurled down. **They overcome him by the blood of the lamb** *and by the word of their testimony; they did not love their lives so much as to shrink from death. Therefore rejoice, you heavens and you who dwell in them!* **But woe to the earth and the sea,** *because the devil has gone down to you! He is filled with fury, because he knows that his time is short.' "*

We can see that the one hurled down was Satan with all his angels. About one third of the angels followed the devil. All were cast out of heaven and placed down at our earth. Here we also can understand the reason for this big scene of war. This is in connection with the victory of Jesus Christ on the cross. With His death and resurrection the salvation was established. But the power and the kingdom of God was also given over to Jesus Christ. He got the authority in His hands. He and His angels won the war against the devil and his angels by the blood of the Lamb. It seems evident that the Michael who was strong enough in verse seven and eight to win over the devil and his angels is the same as Jesus Christ in verses 10–12. The victorious Michael is Jesus Christ himself. The reason for the victory and the event for it is Jesus' death and resurrection. They overcome the devil by the blood of the Lamb. To show when this happened, let us read from John 12:31–33, just after Jesus was glorified:

" '*Now is the time for* **judgment** *on this world;* **now the prince of this world will be driven out.** *But I, when I am lifted up from the earth, will draw all men to myself.' He said this to show what kind of death he was going to die.*"

This text tells us when the devil was judged and when he was driven out. He was judged when Jesus was lifted up on the cross, since the last text mentions His death. So with the victory on the cross, the devil had to leave his place. Since He still is in this world, it must have been heaven that he had to leave. This is, of course, in full harmony with Revelation Chapter 12. Thus the blood of the

Lamb is the big victory. With this achievement, all other events are small, not insignificant, but of lesser importance. If Jesus Christ had not been victorious, there would have been no salvation for sinners. With that, no hope for the world and the devil and his angels possibly could live forever. Everything was at stake with this event. Can you imagine that if Jesus had sinned only one time, everything would have been in vain? If you connect this with the war in heaven with billions and billions of angels, this easily could be the connection we need in Daniel 12 verse one. The time of distress such as has not happened from the beginning of the nations until then could very well be this event described in Revelation 12. With this, the accuser did not have access to heaven as he had in the days of Job.

In the text from Revelation and the gospel of John, we got the definition of who Michael is, namely, Jesus Christ. We also saw that the war in heaven is very likely the same as the time of distress mentioned in Daniel, Chapter 12.

THE DELIVERANCE OF "YOUR" PEOPLE...

With this knowledge of Michael being Jesus Christ Himself and the big distress being the battle for the dominion of all the universe, let us now go on in Chapter 12 of Daniel to see how it fits. In the last part of verse 1 and in verses 2–3 we read:

> *"...**But at that time your people**—everyone whose name is found written in the book—**will** be **delivered**. Multitudes who sleep in the dust of the earth will awake: some to everlasting life, others to shame and everlasting contempt. Those who are wise **will** shine like the brightness of the heavens and those who lead many to righteousness, like the stars for ever and ever."*

Jesus will arise and at that time there will be a distress as never seen before. Finally, with the victory on the cross, the act of salvation was performed and established. This act actually delivered all God's children from death.

Everything is already accomplished. This act is the guarantee for our forgiveness of sins and the gift of salvation. We need to say yes or no to this offer. The text does not say that the saints came to heaven at this moment. It actually says that with this distress and victory in history they will be delivered, they will awake, they will shine and so on. It is a promise which will be fulfilled at the end of age, which is the same as His second coming. If you see these first verses in Daniel Chapter 12 as a promise, you really can find these verses to be the gospel in the Book of Daniel. Let us continue to read from verse 4:

> *"But you, Daniel, close up and **seal the words** of the **scroll until** the time of **the end**. Many will go here and there to increase knowledge."*

This verse does not say that the events described above will happen at the end of the time. What it says is that the understanding of these verses will be closed up until the time of the end. At the time of the end we will understand. If you believe that we now live in this time of the end, then it is the time for us to pray for wisdom and understanding about these verses. Let us continue to read verses 5–7:

> *"Then I Daniel, looked, and there before me stood two others, one on this bank of the **river** and one on the opposite bank. One of them said to the man **clothed in linen**, who was above the waters of the river, **'How long will it be before these astonishing things are fulfilled?'** The man clothed in linen, who was above the waters of the river, lifted his right hand and his left hand toward heaven, and I heard him swear by him who lives forever, saying, **'It will be for a time, times and half a time. When the power of the holy people has been finally broken, all these things will be completed.'"***

The river and its banks were first mentioned in Daniel 10:4. As you might know, Chapters 10–12 are explanation for the same vision. Daniel was standing on the bank of Tigris. In verse 5 we read:

*"I looked up and there before me was a **man dressed in linen**, with a belt of the finest gold around his waist."*

There is a close connection to the vision starting in Chapter 10. We find the river with its banks but also the man dressed in linen. It seems to be the same heavenly being. In verse six of Chapter 12 we read the question: "How long will it be until these astonishing things are fulfilled?" What things is Daniel thinking about? The only issue we have found so far is the period of big distress from verse one and the promises connected to it. That means his actual question is: "How long will this big time of distress last?" The answer is: "It will be for a time, times and a half time." Please do also notice how the answer is said. It does not say: "After three and a half times" or "It will start after three and a half times." However, it says: "It will be for three and a half times." It will be is the same as: "This situation of distress will last for three and a half times." One time in the Bible is usually one year. That means it will be for three and a half years. Do you see? The biggest time of distress during the whole history will be Jesus' three and a half years' mission on earth from His baptism in Jordan up till His dying on the cross followed by His resurrection. The whole universe followed intensely to see if Jesus would be victorious or not. We know the wonderful answer, that Jesus won on the cross. When this time of distress or war in heaven was over, the accuser and his angels were the losers and subsequently hurled down to the earth. All this was accomplished through the blood of the Lamb.

THE POWER OF THE HOLY PEOPLE...

The heavenly being continues to give us a clue when it will happen. In the last part of verse 7 we read:

*"When the **power of the holy people** has been **finally broken**, all these things will be completed."*

Whenever the "power of the holy people has been finally broken," it will be fulfilled or "completed." What is the understanding of the power of the holy people? When was it broken? Whatever it may be, it must happen around the time of Jesus dying on the cross. Is there such an event? Let us read from Ephesians 2:14–18:

> *"For He himself is our peace, who has made the two one and has **destroyed the barrier, the dividing wall of hostility**, by abolishing in His flesh the law with its commandments and regulations. His purpose was to **create in Himself one** new man out of the two, thus making peace, and in this one body to **reconcile both of them to God through the cross**, by which he put to death their hostility. He came and preached peace to you who were far away and peace to those who were near. For through Him we both have access to the Father by one Spirit."*

Before the cross there was Israel, chosen by God, and the Gentiles. That we can understand if we read verses 12–13 in the same Chapter 2 in Ephesians:

> *"Remember that at that time you were **separate from Christ, excluded from** citizenship in Israel and foreigners to **the covenants of the promise**, without hope and **without God** in the world. But now in Christ Jesus you who once were far away have been brought near through **the blood of Christ.**"*

Between the chosen Israel and the Gentiles there were, sad to say, dividing walls, barriers and even hostility. After the cross there is only one body. So with the cross, we can see that the last part of verse seven in Daniel 12 is fulfilled. The power of the holy people or the favoritism was broken on the cross. After the cross, there is one body of believers, not two. If this is the fulfillment of when the power of the holy people is broken, then we will also understand that this is the time when "all these things will be completed." What is meant with all these things? Probably Daniel is thinking about what is happening in verses 11–12. We will look at that shortly. Now let us continue to read from verse 8:

> *"I heard, but I did not understand. So I asked, 'My lord, what will the outcome of all this be?' "*

If you do not understand, you try to ask another question. This is exactly what Daniel did. Let us see what the answer is. We read verse 9 and 10:

> *"He replied, "Go your way, Daniel, because **the words are closed up and sealed** until the **time of the end.** Many will be **purified,** made spotless and refined, but the wicked will continue to be wicked. None of the wicked will understand, but those who are wise will understand."*

First the angel says no and reminds Daniel that the words are sealed to the time of the end. Notice, it does not say that the event will take place at the time of the end. The understanding of the words will be unsealed to the wise and this will happen at the time of the end. However, the angel gives us still some further comments. Many will be purified and spotless, etc. Remember we are still talking about the big time of distress which is ended with Christ's victory on the cross. And, of course, it is through Him and only through His victory on the cross we can be made pure, spotless and refined. Since not everyone accepts Christ, the rest will continue to be wicked.

THE DAILY SACRIFICE...

We are now approaching the main message of this vision. At the same time, this is one of the most difficult passages to understand. If you look at different translations, you will find a big variation, probably because many are unsure what to do with this passage. Let us first read from verses 11–12:

> *"From the time that the **daily sacrifice is abolished** and the **abomination that causes desolation is set up,** there will be **1,290 days.** Blessed is the one who reaches the **end of the 1,335 days."***

Here are three components we need to solve: (1) The daily sacrifice being abolished. (2) What is abomination and how to set it up. (3) The meaning of the word "desolation." After that is accomplished, we must be able to put all three things together in a sound biblical way and have it match the rest of the book of Daniel and the Bible as a whole. Let us first look at number one. When was the daily sacrifice abolished and what does it mean? For the first question there are two answers. For those of you who are good in history, we know that the temple was destroyed AD 70. When the temple was destroyed at AD 70, there was one possible fulfillment of this prophecy. The temple was destroyed and profaned by the Roman empire. There is no historical question about that event. It really took place. If we believe this option, we have a problem. As you will see later on in the study of Chapter 9, the same events are mentioned. In Daniel 9:27 we find: (1) Put an end to sacrifice and offering. (2) Set up abomination. (3) Something about the word "desolation." In Chapter 9, all these events have to fit within the 490-year period ending 34 AD. Is it then tolerable to say that Chapter 12, with the same events, will end after 34 AD, in AD 70 or at the end of age? Of course not! There must be harmony between the parts of the Bible, at least with Chapters 9 and 12, which seem to be very close.

If we leave option 1 for a moment and turn our eyes to the other option, the second possibility is the event that took place at the death of Jesus on the cross. Let us look at this option. When Jesus died, we all know that the curtain in the temple was destroyed. In Matthew 27:51–52 we read:

> "At that moment the **curtain of the temple was torn** in two from top to bottom. The tombs broke open and the bodies of many holy people who had died were raised to life."

Here it is shown that the dividing wall was gone and the way was now open from the Holy place to the Most Holy Place. If we look at the sacrifice system in the Old

Testament, we find that atonement was achieved once a year. At that time, the high priest went in from the holy place to the most holy place and atoned for the people. No one other than the high priest was allowed to enter the most holy place. We also know that the sacrificial system was an image of the real sacrifice, Jesus Christ dying on the cross. So when Jesus Christ died and the curtain to the most holy place tore, this is an indication of the successful sacrifice of Messiah on the cross. Also notice that the curtain tore from top to bottom, which could emphasize that it was not done by a human hand but an act done of God. Let us read from Hebrew 9:12:

> *"He (Jesus) did not enter by means of the blood of goats and calves; but* **he entered the Most Holy Place once for all by His own blood**, *having obtained eternal redemption."*

Taking both texts together, it shows that the daily sacrifice system was abolished with the sacrifice of Jesus Christ. Regardless when the sacrifice system in the Jewish system was stopped, it was meant to be terminated when Jesus died on the cross when He once and for all went into the Most Holy Place. This was accomplished when the curtain was torn from top to bottom. If we now read Daniel 9:25–27, the picture will be more clear:

> *"Know and understand this: From the issuing of the decree to restore and rebuild Jerusalem until the Anointed One, the ruler comes, there will be seven 'sevens,' and sixty-two 'sevens.' It will be rebuilt with streets and a trench, but in times of trouble. After the sixty-two 'sevens,' the* **Anointed One will be cut off and will have nothing**. *The people of the ruler who will come will destroy the city and the sanctuary. The end will come like a flood: War will continue until the end, and desolations have been decreed. He will confirm a covenant with many for one 'seven.'* **In the middle of the 'seven' He will put an end to sacrifice and offering**. *And on the wing of the temple he will set*

*up an abomination that causes desolation, until
the end that is decreed is poured out on him."*

Here we can see how well it fits to the Anointed One,
who is Christ, and how he was cut off. The last expression
is the same as to be killed. In the next verse, we also recognize how the sacrifice and offering system was put to
an end in the "middle" of the last "seven" prophecy. This
is again the time of death on the cross. Another interesting aspect of this is Jesus' own view on this. When Jesus
talked to the disciples about His upcoming death, He said
that the temple would be destroyed and in three days rebuilt again. Everybody thought He was crazy because they
were thinking of the Temple built of stones. This temple
took many years to build. But Jesus said it would be rebuilt again in three days. You can read the story in John
2:18–21:

> *"Then the Jews demanded of Him, 'What miracu-
> lous sign can you show us to prove your authority
> to do all this?' Jesus answered them, **'Destroy this
> temple, and I will raise it again in three days.'**
> The Jews replied, 'It has taken forty-six years to
> build this temple, and you are going to raise it in
> three days?' **But the temple He had spoken of was
> His body."***

The Israelites made the same mistake as we often do.
What if Daniel 12:11–12 is meant to be spiritual and not
literal! So far we have seen that the abolishing of the sacrifice could very easily mean Jesus' death on the cross.
This makes sense. It is the most victorious moment in
world history. This historic event is now the base for other
events. If we now go back to verse 11 in Daniel Chapter
12, we see that there is a time period starting from the
abolishing of the sacrifice until the next event will take
place. There will be 1,290 days from the time the sacrifice was abolished up till the abomination is set up.

ABOMINATION...

After the time period of 1,290, the abomination that

causes desolation will take place. If this is 1,290 years, we will end up around 1,321 AD. If it is meant to be days, we will end up about three and a half years and one month after Christ's death. Before we look into this time period of 1,290 days, let us take a closer look at the word "abomination." The word "abomination" can be found in Isaiah 66:17:

> *"'Those who consecrate and purify themselves to go into the gardens, following the one in the midst of those who **eat the flesh of pigs and rats and other abominable things**—they will meet their end together,' declares the LORD."*

And in Jeremiah Chapter 32 and verse 34 we read:

> *"They **set up their abominable idols in the house that bears my Name and defiles it**."*

Abominable things are used for many things from unclean animals up to anything that is an idol. In the last text from Jeremiah, the word abominable is used in connection with God's temple. These idols in the house of the Lord are mentioned to be abominable by the Lord. The worst thing an Israelite could do was to put something unholy in the Temple or connect it to the function of the sacrificial system. This shows how the word "abomination" was used to mean something very bad in the eyes of our Lord. Another word used to explain the same thing is the word "detestable." However, it appears safe to use the word "unholy" instead of abominable, and then we can more easily understand the use of the word.

DESOLATION...

The word "desolation" has several meanings, but most often it means uninhabited with regards to people, animals, houses or vegetation. Interestingly enough, there are a few verses with a different meaning or, better said, a deeper meaning. In Leviticus 26:34–35 and verse 43 we read:

"Then the **land will enjoy its Sabbath years** *all the time* **that it lies desolate** *and you are in a country of your enemies; then the land will have the rest and enjoy its Sabbaths. All the time that it lies desolate, the land* **will have the rest it did not have during the Sabbaths you lived in it***"*

"For the land will be **deserted** *by them and will enjoy its Sabbaths while it lies* **desolate** *without them. They* **will pay for their sins** *because they* **rejected my laws and abhorred my decrees.***"*

Here we see that desolation is used in connection with a punishment from the Lord due to sin and rejection of the law. Since the Sabbath law was violated for many years, the country was forced into rest. The country was deserted or made desolate. This translation is very interesting; and let us continue to the following. Let us now read Isaiah 62:4–5 and we will see another aspect of the word "desolation."

"No longer will they call you **Deserted**, *or name your land* **Desolate**. *But you will be called Hephzibah, and your land Beulah;* **for the LORD will take delight in you, and your land will be married.** *As a young man marries a maiden, so will your sons marry you; as a bridegroom rejoices over his bride,* **so will God rejoice over you.***"*

In this context, "deserted" and "desolate" stand in opposition to "married." To be desolate is the same as unmarried or alone. That context we find, for example, in 2 Samuel 13. Here Tamar was raped by her brother Amnon. When that was discovered, Amnon's brother Absalom took care of his sister. In verse 20 we read:

"...And Tamar lived in her brother Absalom's house, a **desolate woman.***"*

She lived in Absalom's house for the rest of her life and was unmarried. She lived alone, without a husband. There are many places in the Bible where Jesus is pictured as the bridegroom and the chosen ones as His bride.

This parable shows the intimate relationship God wants to have with His people. That is why God wants to use the picture of marriage in connection with His people. In Jeremiah 3:14 we read:

> *"'Return, faithless people,' declares the LORD, 'for I am your **husband**.'"*

The chosen people of God is His bride. This picture tells us further that the relationship can be broken if the bride persistently rebels against the bridegroom with adultery. In Hosea 1:2 and 9:15 we read:

> *"because the land is **guilty** of the **vilest adultery** in departing from the **LORD**."*

> *"Because of their sinful deeds, I will **drive them out of my house**."*

Adultery or prostitution are words used for worshipping idols. If the marriage is broken by adultery, a separation or divorce would take place and the consequences would be the same as desolation or desertion. In Isaiah 54:1 (which is also quoted in Galatiens 4: 27) and Hosea 2:23 we read:

> *"Sing, O barren woman, you who never bore a child; burst into song, shout for joy, you who were never in labor; because **more are the children of the desolate woman** than of her who has a husband, says the **LORD**."*

> *"I will say to those called 'Not my people,' 'You are my people.' "*

In this context we get a wonderful understanding of the whole picture. The Lord has very few children or believers among his chosen people. In the Old Testament days, they were the Israelites. On the contrary He had many more children with the nonmarried woman, the woman who never had labor pain or never delivered children by birth. This means God had many more believers outside His chosen people than inside. Those people who always were called "not my people" will get a change in status. They will, from a certain point in time, be called "my people" by the Lord. And please notice that God has not been unfaithful with the desolate woman. She is unmarried and has never borne a child or been in labor pain. These children are probably adopted and accepted by grace. In the parable of the wedding banquet in Matthew 22, you can read the same story. From verse 2–10 we read:

> *"The kingdom of heaven is like a king who prepared a wedding banquet for his son. He sent his servants* **to those who had been invited** *to the banquet to tell them to come,* **but they refused to come***. Then he sent some more servants... but they paid not attention and went off—one to his field, another to his business. The rest seized his servants, mistreated them and killed them. The king was enraged. He sent his army and destroyed those murderers and burned their city. Then he said to his servants, 'The wedding banquet is ready, but those invited did not deserve to come. Go to the street corners and invite to the banquet anyone you find.'* **So the servants went out into the streets and gathered all the people they could find, both good and bad***, and the wedding hall was filled with guests."*

In this parable of Jesus we find the same story. Those initially invited refused to come to the banquet. After several trials, the king finally decided to invite anyone on the streets, regardless if they were considered good or bad in some people's eyes. These words good and bad might have caused confusion. But this was not meant to change the wedding entrance criteria, since in verse 12 we clearly see that the wedding guests needed to have the wedding clothes on. Without wedding clothes, which must be Christ's righteousness, they were thrown outside. This picture shows that when the chosen Israelites refused to come, God turned the invitation to the Gentiles, who actually were considered "bad" in the eyes of Israel. Think, for example, about the Israelites' attitude towards the

Samaritans. Consider also the words of Jesus Himself in Matthew 23:37–38:

> *"O Jerusalem, Jerusalem, you who kill the prophets and stone those sent to you, how often I have longed to gather your children together, as a hen gathers her chicks under her wings, **but you were not willing. Look, your house is left to you desolate.**"*

Jesus is here announcing the consequences of Israel's actions. You have not been willing to be my children. Jesus, in His love, wanted to gather all His children into His family and under the protection of His wings. He is really pouring out His love to them by saying; "How often have I longed." He is really showing the long-lasting mercy and patience to the Israelites. Eventually, He has to give up and announce the consequences. Since "you are not willing," the outcome will be seen. Your house, which here means the house of Israel, "will be left desolate." He has to divorce them as His chosen people. In Romans 7:2 we can read about another reason for divorce:

> *"For example, by law a married woman is bound to her husband as long as he is alive, but if her **husband dies,** she is **released from the law of marriage.**"*

With this text we now have found two reasons for divorce, according to the Bible. One is adultery and the other one is death. In the first case with adultery, it is hard to realize that a loving God can come to an end with His love and be ready for a divorce. Even if many texts have this picture in the Bible, it is probably more a way of showing the possible consequences and rights a husband has. In this case the Lord's rights are shown in the aspect of a husband's relations towards His people. The second reason for divorce is more easy to understand. If the husband dies, the wife is free. This reason for divorce has absolutely no negative impacts. The husband is dead. In this case Jesus is dead, and His bride is free. The wonderful good news is, however, that after His resurrection, He is willing to adopt His children by grace both from the Jews and the Gentiles. He wants to adopt children both from His first marriage and from all the Gentiles, who previously were outside the covenant. This reason is the most likely and with His death, His love can be broadened to many more. The wonderful news is that God is not the limitation in this new covenant. We alone are the limitation. Either we accept God's grace or not. God has, as always, fulfilled His part.

1,290 DAYS...

As you began to see, the understanding of the word "desolate" is very important. With this background, we now will return to Daniel 12:11. At the cross of Jesus and at the time of His death, He divorced His people, His bride, the Israelites. The Israelites could not continue to be His chosen people. Let us now go back to our text in Daniel 12:11:

> "From the time that the **daily sacrifice is abolished**
> and the **abomination that causes desolation is set
> up**, there will be **1,290 days.**"

At AD 31 Jesus died on the cross, and with that He was no longer the husband to the Israelites. The legal divorce according to the law was fulfilled. Now the next question will be, when were the Gentiles accepted? According to the text above, 1,290 days will pass, and then the abomination will be set up. That means the Gentiles will be accepted 1,290 days after the death on the cross. When Stephen was stoned, step two in this process was fulfilled. God not only divorced His bride, but He also accepted the unholy, the primarily nonchosen, the Gentiles. In other words, the abomination is set up. This means full acceptance of the unholy woman, the unmarried woman. The unmarried woman or the Gentiles were now adopted instead of the Israelites. This is very likely the meaning of the phrase "the abomination that causes desolation is set up," as we have read in Daniel 12 and verse

11. Please read the following texts from the New Testament:

Acts 18:6

"But when the Jews opposed Paul and became abusive, he shook out his clothes in protest and said to them, 'Your blood be on your own heads! I am clear of my responsibility. **From now on I will go to the Gentiles.***'"*

Romans 11:5

"...there is a **remnant** *chosen by* **grace.***"*

Romans 11:11

"...because of their transgression, salvation has come to the Gentiles."

If we rephrase verse 11 in Chapter 12 of Daniel, we will find the following: "From the time that the daily sacrifice is abolished (Christ's death on the cross) and the abomination (the unholy) that causes desolation (the unmarried woman/Gentiles) is set up, there will be 1,290 days." These days represent 3 and $\frac{1}{2}$ years plus one month, to be very accurate. We know from Daniel, Chapter 9, that Messiah will be killed in the middle of the last "seven," lasting from AD 27 to AD 34. Thus, He will be killed AD 31. With this accuracy we can feel comfortable unless someone very specialized in history can count the exact days between Jesus dying on the cross and the stoning of Stephen. With good probability, this time period of 1,290 days is this second part of the last "seven," mentioned in Daniel Chapter 9.

1,335 DAYS...

After the 1,290 days, there seems to be some bad times. It does not explicitly say so, but in the next following sentence we get this understanding. As we read above, it says in Daniel 12:3 that "blessed is the one who waits for and reaches the end of the 1,335 days." This means that there probably was something non-blessing or non-pleasant happening before the 1,335 days. There is a time period of 45 days between 1,290 and 1,335 days. But after 1,335 days, there will be blessings, something to wait for. What could that be? If we now look into the history of Acts, we can read from Acts 8:1:

> "On **that day** a **great prosecution** broke out against the church at Jerusalem, and all except the apostles were **scattered** throughout Judea and Samaria."

We can here see the first Christian persecution take place. It started the same day that Stephen was stoned and consequently the same day Gentiles were adopted. The Christians were spread to Judea and Samaria. In Acts 8:14, 17 we read:

> "When the apostles in Jerusalem heard that **Samaria had accepted the word of God**, they sent Peter and John to them. Then Peter and John placed their hands on them, and **they received the Holy Spirit**."

This is really a new event in the church history. The Samarians are not only receiving Jesus Christ as their Messiah but also receiving the Holy Spirit. The Samarians, who have been considered despised and rejected, are now believers and filled with the Spirit of God. Could this be the blessing we should look forward to in Daniel Chapter 12:12? Let us look further. In the last part of Chapter 8 in Acts, we see the conversion and baptism of the Ethiopian eunuch. This again is wonderful news and shows the opening of the gospel to the African continent. In Chapter 9 of Acts we have the dramatic conversion of Saul; and through this event eventually a tremendous growth of the Christian church took place through him in the whole known world at that time. Another example of blessing we find in Acts, Chapter 10 and verses 11–13, where we read about Peter's vision.

> "He saw heaven opened and something like a large sheet being let down to earth by its four corners. It

*contained **all kinds of** four-footed animals, as well as reptiles of the earth and the birds of the air. Then a voice told him, 'Get up, Peter. **Kill and eat.**'"*

And we all know the end of the story. The Holy Spirit soon thereafter fell on Cornelius and his house, and in Chapter 11 we have the conference in Jerusalem deciding what to do about these developments. The final comments after hearing Peter's whole story, we can read in Acts 11:18:

> *"When they heard this, they had no further objections and praised God, saying, '**So then, God has granted even the Gentiles repentance unto life.**' "*

The falling of the Holy Spirit in Samaria, the baptism of the Ethiopian eunuch, Saul's conversion and the general acceptance of the Gentiles as Christians are four examples coming right after the stoning of Stephen and the initial persecution. These events are described in the three following chapters right after the death of Stephen. We do not know how many days passed since the stoning of Stephen until these events, but it seems possible to happen during a short time of days rather than years. There is a time of 45 days from 1,290 till 1,335. These four episodes mentioned above were all happening to open the way for salvation to the Gentiles. Up to this point, the early Christians were mainly converted Israelites. With this step the hostility was gone, the dividing walls were broken, as we read in Ephesians 2:14–18. In the power of the cross, all people, both Israelites and Gentiles, were reconciled and brought to peace in Christ. At the same time the whole world was opened as a mission field. So we can really join Daniel in his praise, "Blessed is the one who reaches the end of the 1,335 days." We all have reason today to be thankful for this blessing which took place soon after the stoning of Stephen.

In Daniel 12:13, which is the last verse, Daniel gets a wonderful promise that he will inherit the kingdom of God. This is an encouraging end of the Book of Daniel.

Starting our study of Daniel with Chapter 12 might have been unusual to you. But now you can see why. The last three chapters of Daniel are rich with detailed information so it is difficult to secure an understanding of Chapter 12. Since this chapter has many strong landmarks, you have already seen that it is possible to explain each verse even if it stands alone. This chapter also tells us that the interpretation of these chapters should be sealed until the time of the end. No one reading this book would have difficulty believing that we live in the end time right now. Otherwise you probably wouldn't read this book. Why God chose to seal this information to the end time, we do not know. Let us see if we now, with this new understanding, can connect Chapter 12 to the rest of the chapters in Daniel. Let us first look at Chapter 9.

Daniel: Chapter 9

THE DESOLATION OF JERUSALEM...

The Babylonian kingdom has been conquered by the Mede and now Darius, son of Xerxes, is king. In his first year of reign, Daniel is studying the Scriptures. In verse 2 we read:

> *"In the first year of his reign, I, Daniel, understood from the Scriptures, according to the word of the LORD given to Jeremiah the prophet, that **the desolation of Jerusalem would last seventy years.**"*

He is obviously reading from Jeremiah and very likely from Chapter 29 and verses 10, 11 and 14:

> *"This is what the LORD says: '**When seventy years are completed for Babylon,** I will come to you and fulfill my gracious promise to bring you back to this place. For I know the plans I have for you,' declares the LORD, 'plans to prosper you and not to harm you, plans to give you hope and a future.'"*

> *"'I will be found by you,' declares the LORD, 'and will bring you back from captivity...and will **bring you back to the place from which I carried you into exile.**'"*

This was the text studied and contemplated. With this knowledge that the captivity would last 70 years and that these 70 years were almost over, Daniel now starts to plead with God in prayer and petition in combination with fasting. He also is wearing sackcloth and ashes. This is Daniel's way of showing sincerity toward God. He is pleading with God from the bottom of his heart. Daniel loves his people and wants to make sure that the promise in Jeremiah will be fulfilled. From verse 4–19 we have his wonderful model prayer and confession. Let us here read a few verses to show some points:

*"O, Lord, the great and awesome God, who keeps his covenant of love with all who love him and obey his commands, we **have sinned** and done wrong. We have **been wicked** and have rebelled; we have **turned away from your commands and laws**. We have **not listened** to your servants the **prophets**....The LORD did not hesitate to bring the disaster upon us, for the LORD our God is righteous in everything He does....For your sake, O LORD, look with favor on your **desolate sanctuary**....O Lord listen! O Lord forgive! O Lord hear and act! For your sake, O my God, do not delay, because **your city and your people bear your Name**."*

If you read the whole prayer you will get a special blessing. Daniel starts the prayer by praising God. It is a humble man's prayer, no boasting at all. He is actually interceding for his people and asking for forgiveness for all their sins. He does not come with excuses. He accepts the sinful situation of his people and wants to have God's mercy. In verse 20 we read that while Daniel was still in prayer and confessing the sins of himself and his people, the angel Gabriel came to see him. In verse 22 and 23 we read:

*"He instructed me and said to me, 'Daniel, I have now come **to give you insight and understanding**. As soon as you began to pray, an answer was given, which I have come to tell you, for you are highly esteemed. Therefore, **consider the message and understand the vision**.'"*

Daniel's prayer was wonderful in many ways and stands as a model for us. Still, it was not the prayer only which gave this response from God. Daniel was considered highly esteemed by God, probably for a long time. Daniel had a wonderful and significant relationship with our Lord. This was surely the reason for the prayer in the first place as well as the reason for the answer. Isn't it awesome to see how quickly God was ready to answer? As Daniel began to pray, the answer was given. I am willing to go even one step further and say: Because of his intimate relationship with God, the Holy Spirit impressed Daniel to pray the right prayer at the right time. The plan was also that Daniel should consider the vision, he should think it over. Maybe he did not understand it right away, but it was meant to be to his understanding. In Chapter 9 it does not say that Daniel saw a vision, but there is an angel coming and giving him understanding.

In Webster, one of the explanations for the word "vision" is "unusual discernment or foresight." In the NIV Concordance by E.W. Goodrick and in the New Strong's Complete Dictionary of Bible Words, the word "mar'eh" is found here. Most often this word is translated to the English word "appearance." That means that the last sentence in verse 23 could have been translated to: "Therefore, consider the message and understand the appearance or foresight." In other words, understand what I, the angel Gabriel, am about to tell Daniel. In Chapter 10:7 it says that Daniel saw the vision. But here in Chapter 9 it does not say he saw a vision, but a message is given to Daniel, since he is able to understand God's plan. When you want someone to understand something, you have to use all your imagination to get out the message. So what is the message and what is the foresight? The initiation for this event is Daniel's prayer about the seventy years in captivity in Babylon. What will happen next is the question in Daniel's mind. And in the next verse, we can clearly see what the message constitutes. The angel starts to talk about the seventy "sevens." This is the message or its appearance. We could also talk about how to understand the foresight the angel is giving Daniel. In clear words, Daniel did not have a dream or vision, which was the case in many other chapters of the book of Daniel. This message is coming as a response to a prayer, where Daniel asks for understanding of the future for his people after the 70 years in captivity are ended.

SEVENTY "SEVENS"...

Then the real message delivered by the angel followed,

and in verse 24 we read:

> *"**Seventy 'sevens'** are decreed for **your people** and your holy city to **finish transgression**, to put an **end to sin**, to **atone for wickedness**, to **bring in everlasting righteousness**, to seal up vision and prophecy and to **anoint the most holy.**"*

Many good books have been written about the meaning of seventy "sevens," and the interpretation of the prophecy does not need to be repeated in full length here. 70 times 7 = 490. In prophetic Scripture one time is a year, which makes this 490 years. So 490 years are decreed for Daniel's people. In the verse it says "your people," and that must be the Israelites. This is not a world history lecture by the angel. This is revelation from God of what He has in mind for the Israelites. That is why the answer is 490 years are for your people, Daniel. But in what aspect? When Peter, the disciple of Jesus, came to Jesus, he asked, how many times I shall forgive my brother when he sins against me? Up to seven times? he asked. The answer of Jesus in Matthew 18:21–22 is not seven times but seventy "seven" times, which is 490 times, the same number, as you can see. This is the model from a merciful God showing the heavenly perspective of forgiving. Jerusalem is now desolate due to sin and transgression. Still God wants to give his chosen people another 490 years to finish transgression and sin. God wants to give Israel a long time period for them to be able to repent and turn back to Him.

YOUR PEOPLE...

Another important finding is how the words "your people" are used. This is the same start as in Daniel 12 and verse 1, where "your people" is mentioned twice. This indicates that both interpretations are for the Israelites, not for anyone else. Both chapters also set the time to finish transgression, sin and wickedness. This must happen within 490 years in Chapter 9 and in Chapter 12 up till the stoning of Stephen. Both prophecies end AD 34. Up to this date, the time period is used to indicate the given time for Israel as a nation. After 490 years something will happen with this so-called "your people." After 490 years the Israelites and their holy city Jerusalem were supposed "to finish transgression." God is always merciful and wants to give them one more chance. The expression "to finish transgression" sounds more like a message for the nation. But the last two comments in this verse point towards our savior, Jesus Christ. To "bring in everlasting righteousness" and "to anoint the most holy" are clear indications pointing to the Messiah. According to this text, Messiah will show up during this time of the prophecy. In verse 25 we read:

> *"Know and understand this: From issuing of the decree to restore and rebuild Jerusalem **until the Anointed One, the ruler, comes**, there will be seven 'sevens,' and sixty-two 'sevens.' It will be rebuilt with streets and a trench, but in times of trouble."*

Again, there is no intention in this book to change any times set. Most authors with good historical knowledge agree that the decree was given by Artaxerxes in 457 BC. 7 + 62 makes 69 and times seven = 483 years and ends with the baptism of Jesus, AD 27. When Jesus was baptized in Jordan by John the Baptist, at that time He was also anointed with the Holy Spirit. The Holy Spirit came upon Him in the shape of a dove.

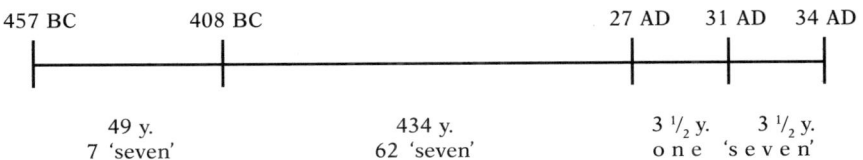

457 BC	408 BC		27 AD	31 AD	34 AD
49 y.	434 y.		3 $\frac{1}{2}$ y.	3 $\frac{1}{2}$ y.	
7 'seven'	62 'seven'		one	'seven'	

The Anointed One, Jesus, is coming as accurately in time as it is possible. But note one thing here! In this translation it says the "Anointed One" and "the ruler" as one and the same. In KJV it says "Messiah the Prince." It strongly supports that Messiah is also "the ruler" in this context. The importance of this, we will see later on. In verse 26 we read:

> *"After the sixty-two 'sevens,' the **Anointed One will be cut off** and will **have nothing**. The **people of the ruler** who will come will **destroy** the city and the **sanctuary**. The end will come like a flood: **War will continue** to the end, and **desolations have been decreed**."*

To be cut off is the same as to be killed. Subsequently we realize that the Messiah will die after AD 27. However, how soon after AD 27 this verse does not say. But please look at our study in the following verses. It was also mentioned that at His death He will have "nothing." To have nothing has probably a multidimensional meaning. When Jesus died at the cross, He was absolutely alone. No one supported Him in His agony. Even His Father left him at that moment. In Matthew 27:46 Jesus cried out:

> *"My God, my God why have you forsaken me?"*

Jesus was carrying all the sin of the world alone. He had nothing to rely on. What a sacrifice! There is also another possible explanation for having "nothing." In Daniel 12 and verse 7 we studied in previous chapters about the three and a half years and then "the power of the holy people has been finally broken." Messiah did not only bear all the sins of the world, but He also divorced His chosen people, His bride. Even in this aspect, He at this moment had nothing. The Israelites refused to accept Him and killed Him. This is exactly what is said in the parable of the wedding banquet in Matthew 22.

In Daniel 9:26 we also read that "the people of the ruler will destroy the city." The Israelites did not literally destroy the city, but due to verse 24 they had 490 years decreed not only for them as a nation but also for the city of Jerusalem to be cleansed and holy. Since it did not happen, Jerusalem was, after Jesus died on the cross, obviously not the chosen city any longer after AD 31. Maybe that is the reason why we will get the "New Jerusalem" from heaven one day, according to Revelation 21.

SANCTUARY AND SACRIFICE...

The same verse in Daniel also tells us that the "people of the ruler will destroy the sanctuary." Some have understood this to be the Roman emperor destroying Jerusalem and the Temple in AD 70. However, looking at the text more carefully, this text is about "your people," which is the people of Daniel and their acting during the 490 years during this time prophecy. This time prophecy ends in AD 34 and does not continue to AD 70. The temple as a building was not directly destroyed by the Israelites, but due to their transgressions they indirectly were responsible for the temple destruction at AD 70. From these perspectives, this prophecy should not be used on the Roman Empire. The people here are meant to be the Israelites, and they were the ones responsible for the crucifixion of Messiah. The killing of the body of Christ is the same as destroying the temple. Remember Jesus' own quotation about His own body as the temple in John 2:18–21:

> *"Then the Jews demanded of Him, 'What miraculous sign can you show us to prove your authority to do all this?' Jesus answered them, **'Destroy this temple, and I will raise it again in three days.'** The Jews replied, 'It has taken forty-six years to build this temple, and you are going to raise it in three days?' **But the temple He had spoken of was His body.**"*

So, very likely, the destroying of the sanctuary by the people of the ruler was meant to be the crucifixion of Messiah. With this interpretation, all events in the prophecy fall within the time of the prophecy. Thus, they occur before AD 34 and not several years later.

JERUSALEM...

So far we have not been dealing with the meaning of Jerusalem. Of course, most times in the Bible, the word "Jerusalem" stands for the city with its buildings and streets, etc. Jerusalem is and was the capitol of the Jewish nation. However, the word "Jerusalem" is also used in a more global sense. It seems that it can be a substitute for the people living there in the whole land. The city Jerusalem is also given attributes which only fit to a human being. In Matthew 23:37–38 we read:

> *"O Jerusalem, Jerusalem, **you who kills the prophets** and stone those sent to you, how often I have longed to gather your children together, as a hen gathers her chicks under her wings, but you were not willing. Look, **your house is left to you desolate.**"*

In this text above it is clear to everyone that a city cannot kill prophets, but those living in the city can. So this verse shows that the word Jerusalem can sometimes be changed or represent the people living there. In USA we often use the same symbol, with our capitol where the government is placed. Thus the word "Washington" can also be meant to represent the whole nation and what it stands for. In the book of Jeremiah we find the connection to the people that God has chosen and to the throne of the Lord. In Jeremiah 3:14, 17 we read:

> *" 'Return, faithless people,' declares **the LORD**, 'for **I am your husband**. I will choose you...' "*

> *"At that time they will call **Jerusalem** The **Throne of the LORD**, and all the nations will gather in Jerusalem to honor the name of the LORD."*

In these texts we see that Jerusalem is the symbol of His chosen people. As long as the Israelites are God's chosen people, Jerusalem will be the throne of God, or the "city of the Great King," as it is said in Matthew 5:34. We have also studied the concept that God marries His people, which finds support in this text. Here the Lord calls Himself "husband" in connection to His people. With these texts and several more, it is easy to see Jerusalem as a symbol for the people living in it.

If we now return to verse 26 in Daniel Chapter 9, we read that the city will be destroyed as well as the sanctuary. As we understood before, this time the prophecy in Chapter 9 ends AD 34. Therefore it cannot be explained by the destruction of the city Jerusalem, built by timber and stones, at AD 70. There must be another meaning of this expression. Otherwise a time prophecy does not make sense. The only way to get this inside the time prophecy is to take this spiritually, since the people living in Israel were not destroyed AD 34. This interpretation finds support in Jesus' own words in Matthew 23:37, which we read above. There it says that the Lord will let the house of Jerusalem be "left to you desolate," with that meaning the divorce of the Israelites as a chosen nation. With this understanding, everything is in harmony within the prophecy and within the time frame of the prophecy as well. In this connection it is very interesting to read about Jesus when He met the Samaritan woman at the well. His disciples have left for the town to buy food, and Jesus starts a conversation with the woman. After a while she realizes that Jesus is a prophet and the discussion is turning to a spiritual communication. In John 4:19–24 we read:

> "'Sir,' the woman said, 'I can see that you are a prophet. Our fathers worshipped on this mountain, but **you Jews claims that the place to worship is in Jerusalem.**' Jesus declared, 'Believe me, woman, a time is coming when you will worship the Father neither on this mountain nor in Jerusalem. You Samaritans worship what you do not know; we worship what we do know, for salvation is from the Jews. **Yet a time is coming and has now come when the true worshipers will worship the Father in spirit and truth,** for they are the kind of worshipers the Father seeks. God is spirit, and his worshipers must worship in spirit and truth.'"

Jesus announces here that Jerusalem has been the place for worship. He also announces a change that will take place. Actually, the last time He mentions this change, He adds that the "time has now come." With the presence of Jesus on this earth, the change has come. Jesus knows very well that He will not live much longer, and with the death on the cross, He will open the way for the conversion of the Gentiles as well as for the conversion of the Jews. He is divorcing a literal people and adopting by grace anyone who believes in Him. Did you notice that in this text there is also another change? Jerusalem, which has been the worship place before, will be changed to something else. It will be changed to worship the Father "in spirit and truth."

Thus, with the acceptance of the Gentiles, not only grace comes in but also a new place of worship. The literal place, Jerusalem, is changed to a spiritual worship in spirit and truth. To give even more understanding to this, the word "spirit" is meant to be the Holy Spirit and the word "truth" is meant to be Jesus Christ Himself. In John 14:6 we read:

*"I am the way and the **truth** and the life."*

Instead of the city Jerusalem, we now have the Holy Spirit and Jesus Christ. With this change, the church of the Lord is not a localized church but a church covering the whole world. Not even a building is necessary. Jesus is the temple. We can worship our Lord in any country in the world, in the air, on the earth or under the water's surface. We can worship him in nature, in the mountains, in any building, in an airplane, car or submarine. No circumstance is a hindrance. With this change God is reaching out to everyone. This is a true unlimited warranty!

WAR OR DISTRESS...

Another fascinating word in verse 26 is the word "war." There it says that "war will continue until the end." End of what? Up till AD 70 there was not a continuation of war. There is only one thing ending in the same verse and that is the ending of the life of Messiah. If that is what is meant, the war will continue until Jesus dies on the cross. But this is exactly the same as we already have studied in Daniel 12:1 about the great distress when Michael will arise. We also studied the war going on in Revelation 12, where it talks about the war in heaven which is finally overcome by the victory through the blood of the Lamb. So this phrase, "war will continue to the end," is likely to be about the biggest spiritual warfare ever going on in this world's history, culminating with the victory on the cross. The last sentence of verse 26 says that "war will continue until desolations have been decreed," which also means up till Messiah's death on the cross. There was no constant war going on until 70 AD, either spiritual or literal. So this text is another reason why the desolation has to do with the cross, with Jesus' body as the temple and not the temple built of stone and the destruction of it in 70 AD. It reinforces what we have studied before. When Jesus died on the cross, He also divorced His chosen people, Israel. The desolation was decreed at the death on the cross. In Daniel 9:27 we further read:

> *"He will confirm a covenant with many for one 'seven.'* ***In the middle of the 'seven' He will put an end to sacrifice and offering.*** *And on the wing of the temple,* ***He will set up an abomination that causes desolation,*** *until the end that is decreed is poured out on Him."*

Jesus' purpose when starting His ministry in AD 27 was to confirm or strengthen the current covenant with Israel. Unfortunately the hearer of His word did not completely accept Jesus on this view. Jesus came to fulfill and make the covenant strong, not the opposite. Read with me in Matthew 5:17

> *"Do not think that I have come to abolish the Law or the Prophets; I have not come to abolish them but to **fulfill** them."*

God on His side has always fulfilled His part of any

covenant with anyone. God is trustworthy. Are you ready to trust His promises? The next sentence in verse 27 of Daniel Chapter 9 shows the timing of His death. In the middle of the last week, He will die. This happened 31 AD. But to be really accurate, it actually does not state His death here, only the change of function due to His death. It says: "He will put an end to sacrifice and offering." When dying on the cross, all requirements were met in Him in regard to sacrifice and offerings. No sacrifices had to be repeated after this. Of course we need to accept Him, but no more blood needs to be shed. We have already studied this in Chapter 12. But let us be reminded of Hebrew 7:27 where we read:

> *" He sacrificed for their sins **once for all** when He offered Himself."*

Jesus died once for all, for you and me, and with this death, "He put an end to sacrifice and offerings." The sacrifice and offerings were supposed to end in the middle of the "seven." That means in the middle of the last seven years of the whole 490-year time prophecy. If you halve 7 years, you get three and a half years. Please notice the time accuracy here. For example, 360 days is a more determined time interval than one year. The mathematical accuracy of 360 days is +/ - half a day, which equals 12 hours. Such a statement is very specific in time. In contrast to this is the accuracy of one year only +/ - a half year, which equals 180 days. This time mentioning one-year interval is therefore not so specified. In the time prophecy used above, it is about years and not days. This fact needs to be considered and fits very well into our study of the 1,290 days in a previous chapter. If you split 7 years, which equals 2,520 days, into two, you get 1,260 days. 1,260 days is three and a half years. 1,260 + 1,260 = 2,520 or three and a half + three and a half = 7 years. With the accuracy in the current prophetic statement, the prophecy is still fulfilled if Jesus died 1,260 or 1,200 and even 1,150 days after His baptism. If we now look at the last part of this three and a half years, the same thing could be said about the length in days. In Chapter 12 we saw that 1,290 days were needed from His death on the cross up till the stoning of Stephen. This prophecy has enough accuracy to allow 1,290 days instead of 1,260 days. Thus, with this time prophecy in Daniel 9 we have full support for the interpretation already made in our study in the end of Chapter 12.

ABOMINATION THAT CAUSES DESOLATION...

The next phrase in verse 27 of Daniel 9 mentions the next step in the meaning of His death. First it talks about a wing of the Temple. A wing is not the main building and it is something you can add on at a later date. The main building of the temple was for the Israelites and the real temple did not have a wing. If the translation from the Hebrew is accurate here, this wing must be an "add-on." This fits well with the new remnant chosen by grace. As we have studied above, you now recognize this statement, too: "He will set up an abomination that causes desolation." He will, in other words, set up the unholy, the Gentiles, according to what we studied in previous chapters. With this we can see how Daniel Chapter 9 and 12 dwell intimately hand in hand. Both chapters are talking about the end time events, however, not of the world but the end of Israel as a chosen nation.

The last sentence of verse 27 mentions "until the end that is decreed is poured out on Him." Yes, it is the same "He" or "Him" through the whole verse, and it is Jesus Himself the book of Daniel is talking about. The end that was decreed and poured out on Him is His death on the cross in the middle of the last week of the prophecy. With this all necessary steps have been taken to spread the gospel from our Lord to all nations of the world. We all are invited to the wedding banquet, as described by Jesus in Matthew Chapter 22. We are all chosen by grace. Again we are able to find the gospel in Daniel but this time in Chapter 9.

Daniel: Chapter 10

This chapter is the starting point for the vision presented in Chapters 11 and 12. The vision itself is not presented here. However, the background to Daniel is given as well as some guidelines for the understanding of the vision. In verse 1–3 we read:

> "*In the third year of Cyrus, king of Persia, a **revelation** was given to Daniel (who was called Belteshazzar). Its message was true and it **concerned a great war**. The **understanding of the message** came to him in a **vision**. At that time I, Daniel, mourned for **three weeks**. I ate no choice food; no meat or wine touched my lips; and I used no lotions at all until the three weeks were over.*"

First we get the time set. The Babylonian kingdom does not exist any longer and is succeeded by the Medes which we read about in Chapter 9 and now by the Persians in Chapter 10. According to the text, it seems as if Daniel first had a revelation. Due to the content, he is very concerned and mourns for three weeks. His concern is the great war, which we already have studied in Daniel Chapter 12. He probably had the fasting and praying attitude, as he usually did when he was hit with a sincere problem. He was obviously very impressed and shaken about the revelation he got. He had no peace and wanted to understand. Then the understanding came to him in a vision. Very likely this vision came at the end of the three weeks. At least it seems to be so according to verses 10–13:

> "*A hand touched me and set me trembling on my hands and knees. He said, 'Daniel, you who are highly esteemed, consider carefully the words I am about to speak to you, and stand up, for I have been sent to you.' And when he said this to me, I stood up trembling. Then he continued, 'Do not be afraid, Daniel. **Since the first day that you set your mind to gain understanding** and to **humble**"*

*yourself before God, your words were heard, and **I** **have come in response** to them. But the prince of the Persian Kingdom resisted me for **twenty-one days**. Then Michael, one of the chief princes, came to help me, because I was detained there with the king of Persia.'"*

In this passage we find that it took 21 days, which is three weeks, for Gabriel to be free from a previous duty to be able to come to Daniel and give the understanding of the vision. This time period is exactly the same time which Daniel fasted and pleaded with God. The whole situation is very similar to the vision in Chapter 9. There in verse three we saw that Daniel pleaded with God in prayer and petition, in fasting and in sackcloth and ashes, until the interpretation was given. Daniel is still highly esteemed by God and he knows how to approach God. Daniel humbles himself before God, here in some form of fasting. Please notice also that Daniel "set his mind to gain understanding." This is a wonderful phrase, indicating his closeness to God. So an angel, supported by Michael (Jesus Christ) is coming to explain the vision. If we now return to verses 4–6 we read:

*"On the twenty-fourth day of the first month, as I was standing on the bank of the great river, the Tigris, I looked up and there before me was **a man dressed in linen**, with a belt of the finest **gold** around his waist. His body was like **chrysolite**, his face like **lightning**, his eyes like **flaming torches**, his arms and legs like the gleam of burnished bronze, and his voice like the **sound of a multitude**."*

This moment described here is very likely the initial vision where Daniel meets a very glorious being. Who could that be? Can we find a similar description anywhere else in the Bible? The first impression is that this is a godly being. There is actually a similar passage in the book of Revelation, and we read from 1:13–15:

*"and among the lampstands was someone 'like a son of man,' dressed in a robe reaching down to his feet and with a **golden sash around his chest**. His head and hair were white like wool, as white as snow, and his eyes were like **blazing fire**. His feet were like **bronze glowing in a furnace**, and his voice was like the sound of **rushing waters**."*

If you look at the description, we find golden clothing around His chest or waist in both instances. His eyes are either flaming torches or like "blazing fire," and there are similar descriptions about His voice. Remember, when you see a heavenly being, it is not easy to describe it in human words. If the passage read in the book of Revelation is Jesus Christ, then it is very possible that the person Daniel saw in his vision was Jesus Christ Himself. In the passage in the book of Revelation, we understand this image to be Jesus revealing His end time message to His end time church through John. In Daniel 10 we have support to believe that Jesus Himself is revealing His end time message to the end time of His chosen people, the Israelites. In Daniel 10:7–9, we read:

*"I, Daniel, was the only one who **saw the vision**; the men with me did not see it, but such terror overwhelmed them that they fled and hid themselves. So I was left alone, gazing at this great vision; I had no strength left, my face turned deathly pale and I was helpless. Then I heard him speaking, and **as I listened to him, I fell into a deep sleep**, my face to the ground."*

Daniel continues to explain what he saw when the vision was revealed to him by Jesus Christ. The story tells us that this is the vision itself described and not the explanation of the vision by the angel. The seeing of Jesus Himself with His message had this tremendous impact on Daniel. But here there is no interpretation. That is why Daniel now is pleading with God for three weeks.

THE UNDERSTANDING...

In verse 14 we now are coming closer to the explanation or the "understanding," as Daniel said. The angel starts to communicate with Daniel. We understand this is the angel's part, even if the transition from the first revelation of Jesus Christ to the explanation of the angel is hard to find. But in verse 15 we see the second time Daniel is bowing his face to the ground:

> *"While he was saying this to me, **I bowed with my face toward the ground** and was speechless."*

With two times bowing down to the ground, we are very likely dealing with two encounters with heavenly beings. The first encounter, we have decided to be Jesus Christ. Do we have a description of the second heavenly being? Yes, and in verse 18 we read:

> *"Again the one who **looked like a man** touched me and gave me strength. 'Do not be afraid, O man highly esteemed,' he said. 'Peace! Be strong now; be strong.'"*

This time the messenger looks like a man, which contradicts strongly the first description. There is also another difference to be noted between the two encounters. When Daniel saw the vision and Jesus Christ, he fell into a deep sleep with his face to the ground. At the second encounter with someone who looked like a man, Daniel bowed down and was speechless. The more you study this chapter, the better you see the two encounters. The angel needs the help of Michael or Jesus Christ to be able to explain for Daniel the previous vision. After 21 days, this was eventually achieved by Michael. Now we have come to the revelation and to the understanding of the vision by the angel. The first sentence of explanation, we find in verse 14:

> *"Now I have come to explain to you what will happen to **your people** in the future, for the vision **concerns a time yet to come**."*

As we have seen before, this vision is about Daniel's people, here called "your people." It does not mention God's people or anyone else. This is about the Israelites. Here we can see the closeness between Chapters 9 and 10–12 again. In all these chapters the messages are about the Israelites. In Daniel 10:20 to 11:1 we read the last verses before the explanation starts:

> "So he said, 'Do you know why I have come to you? Soon I will return to fight against the prince of Persia, and when I go, the prince of Greece will come; but first I will tell you what is written in the **Book of Truth**. (No one supports me against them except **Michael, your Prince**. And in the first year of Darius the Mede, I took my stand to support and protect him.)'"

The last sentence is the identification of this messenger. The vision Daniel had in the first year of Darius the Mede was his vision about the seventy "sevens" in Chapter 9. In verse 15 we read his name to be the angel "Gabriel." This angel seems to be very powerful and is following Christ when He is on duty. Another fascinating comment is made when the angel refers to Michael as Daniel's Prince. The prince of Persia is not the real prince of Daniel. Yes, he is currently employed by the prince of Persia, but for Daniel there is only one Higher Power. For sure, the Son of God is the prince of Daniel. What a compliment to hear that you are worshipping the true God from God's own messenger. This passage also talks about the Book of Truth. In John 14:6 we read:

> "I am the way and the **truth** and the life. No one comes to the Father except through me."

Consequently this could be from the "Book" about Jesus Christ and His actions. We have already found out that the initial revelation was made by the Truth Himself. And in verse 2 we read that this revelation was true. This word "true" could indicate both the content and the Origin. This revelation is about Jesus Christ but also from

Him. With Jesus' comment above, we have the possibility to put the word of "Jesus" in the context instead of the word "truth."

Daniel: Chapter 11

From verse 2 to the very end of the book of Daniel, we are dealing with the interpretation of one and the same vision. The vision was experienced in Chapter 10, but first in Chapter 11 we get to know the content. Before the angel's message, the importance of this vision is established by having Jesus Christ show up in the vision. Let us now go into the specific explanation Gabriel is giving. In verse 2 we read:

*"Now then, I tell you the **truth**:"*

This is unusual. Of course, you would say, every prophecy in the Bible is telling the truth. That is surely a valid point. The Bible is trustworthy. But maybe the angel wants to convey something deeper. This prophecy is about the end but even more about the Truth Himself, Jesus Christ. We have already studied Chapter 12 and seen the wonderful connection to Chapter 9. And both chapters are deeply involved in the life and action of Christ. This is probably another way of pointing out the goal of this vision, the goal Jesus Christ. In the rest of verse 2 through 4 we read:

*"Three more kings will appear in **Persia**, and the fourth, who will be far richer than all the others. When he has gained power by his wealth, he will stir up everyone against the kingdom of **Greece**. Then a mighty king will appear, who will rule with treat power and do as he pleases. After he has appeared, his empire will be broken up and **parceled out towards the four winds of heaven**. It will not go to his descendants, nor will it have the power he exercised, because his empire will be uprooted and given to others."*

As you can see, the vision has similarities to Chapters 2, 7, and 8. We see the same order of kingdoms. Why is the Bible repeating itself? There is a good reason for it.

Every vision has a specific touch and direction, just like the four gospels. Chapter 2 shows the whole world's history from Babylon and King Nebuchadnezzar all the way to the second coming of Jesus. If you, however, compare Chapter 2 with the start of this vision in Chapter 11, you are amazed right away at how detailed the prophecy is. It does not say one world power is followed by another world power and so on. It really goes into each king. Later on you will find some kings described even more extensively. So we can already summarize that this prophecy in Chapter 11 is very detailed. Subsequently, the biggest mistake we can make is to run too quickly in history in regard to the time of this explanation. Why should a detailed prophecy make jumps of a thousand years or so? It does not make sense. Those big "jumps" we rather anticipate to find in Chapter 2, covering the whole world's history in a few verses. That means the historical route will be the important way for our study. We already have seen that Chapter 12 starts with the baptism of Jesus, so there will our goal be, towards the end of Chapter 11.

Verse two of Chapter 11 talks about the kingdom of Persia and about their four kings. No names are given here, but at least we learn that the fourth of the Persian kings is far richer than the other three. The next verse is about Greece, and there we find the first big king described. There is no question about who it is. It must be Alexander the Great. He was very powerful and conquered the world rapidly. At the peak of his victories, something tragic happened. He died very young, in his early thirties. His kingdom was not given to any relatives but was divided into four parts and given one to each general, everything according to the Bible text.

When Greece was declining, there were two substantial divisions. Towards the north there was Syria, including Babylon, and towards the south we had Egypt. In Syria there was a king named Seleucus I, and the dynasty was named Seleucids, and it is probably referring to him when, in verse 6, it mentions "the king of the north." In Egypt the king was Ptolemy I, and his dynasty was named

Ptolemies, and he is named "the king of the south" in verse 5. If you have more historical interest, please look up historical books. The king of the south and the king of the north continue to be described from verse 5 all the way to verse 16. It is obvious that the angel's explanation is more and more detailed. That is a sign for us not to run too quickly in the history of our interpretation.

THE ROMAN EMPIRE...

From verse 16 and onwards we are facing a new word. Earlier in this chapter we talked about the king of the North and the South. But from here on we have someone called "the Invader." Most commentators agree that we now are dealing with Imperial Rome. In verse 16 we read:

> *"The **invader** will do as he pleases; no one will be able to stand against him. **He will establish himself in the Beautiful Land** and will have the power to destroy it."*

When someone does as he pleases, he must have a lot of power. The next sentence emphasizes that again. No power on this earth can be compared to this power. We also know that the Roman Empire incorporated the land of Israel. Of course it had the strength to destroy the Holy Land, but it did not do that during the time of this prophecy. The text actually is more in agreement with occupation of the Beautiful Land. Israel was not destroyed 34 AD but in AD 70. The first Roman emperor is then described in verses 17–19. The historical expertise tells us that this "king" must have been Julius Caesar. Especially the comments about the daughter and the alliance with the king of the South fit well with Julius Caesar and Cleopatra.

In verse 20 we read about the successor to Julius Caesar. He was Caesar Augustus. He reigned from 31 BC until 14 AD. He is characterized by the angel to be responsible for the first tax collection. We read:

> *"His successor will **send out a tax collector** to*

maintain the royal splendor. In a few years, however, he will be destroyed, yet not in anger or in
battle."

This tax we know the best from Luke Chapter 2. Let
us read from verse 1–2:

"In those days **Caesar Augustus** *issued a decree
that a census should be taken of the entire Roman
world.* **This was the first census...**"

And we know that due to this census, Joseph and Mary
went to Bethlehem in Judea from Nazareth in Galilee. We
also realize that with this act, another prophecy would be
fulfilled. Jesus was then born in Bethlehem and not in
Nazareth. It is amazing that this census by a heathen nation took place. The devil probably did everything he could
to destroy this plan, but he was not successful. We can
again see that God is the strongest force in world history,
not only in spiritual history but in all history. This tax
caused the Savior to be born in Bethlehem because the
implementation of the tax was exactly on time according
to God's plan. Imagine if the tax had come only a short
time later and the Messiah had not been born at the right
place. God's plan is perfect and it is for sure coming true.
We also know that Caesar Augustus died of an illness,
thereby fulfilling the last part of the verse above, that he
should not die of anger or in a battle. He died August 19,
AD 14.

The next emperor after Caesar Augustus was Tiberius.
He reigned from 14 AD to 37 AD. That means he was the
emperor during Jesus' mission on this world. He is the
one in charge of the Roman empire and Israel during the
baptism of Jesus, the crucifixion and during the end of
the prophecy in 34 AD. According to Chapter 11 in Daniel,
he is the last emperor described. From verse 21 all the
way to the last, verse 45, it only talks about "he." No successor is mentioned. And why should it? The time prophecy ends 34 AD and Tiberius reigns to 37 AD. Since Chapter 12 starts with the arising of Michael or Jesus Christ,
this period should be covered. That is why the first verse

of Chapter 12 starts with the words "At that time..." To really get a feeling for the last part of Chapter 11, we will read it in a different way. We read from 21–45; and every time this king is mentioned, we start reading the word "he" from the very left. With this presentation, it is easy to see that the whole passage is about the same emperor. There is no room for a change of person. Caesar Tiberius was adopted by Caesar Augustus. That is why he was not said to be royal:

> "He (Caesar Augustus) will be succeeded by a **contemptible person (Tiberius)** who has not been given the honor of royalty.
>
> He will invade the kingdom when its people feel secure, and
>
> he will seize it through intrigue. Then an overwhelming army will be swept away before him, both it and a prince of the covenant will be destroyed. After coming to an agreement with him,
>
> he will act deceitfully, and with only a few people
>
> he will rise to power. When the richest province feel secure,
>
> he will invade them and will achieve what neither his fathers nor his forefathers did.
>
> He will distribute plunder, loot and wealth among his followers.
>
> He will plot the overthrow of fortresses—but only for a time. With a large army
>
> he will stir up his strength and courage against the king of the South.
>
> his heart will be set against the holy covenant.
>
> He will take action against it...
>
> he will invade the South again,
>
> he will lose heart.
>
> He will return and show favor to those who forsake the holy covenant.

His armed forces will rise up to desecrate the temple fortress and will abolish the daily sacrifice. Then they will set up the abomination that causes desolation. With flattery

he will corrupt those who have violated the covenant...

He will exalt and magnify himself above every god...

He will be successful until the time of wrath is completed...

He will show no regard for the gods of his fathers...

he will honor a god of fortress...

he will honor with gold and silver...

He will attack the mightiest fortresses...

He will invade many countries...

He will also invade the Beautiful Land.

He will extend his power over many countries...

He will pitch his royal tents between the seas at the beautiful holy mountain. Yet

he will come to his end, and no one will help him."

Since this Chapter 11 from verse 21–45 is the same Emperor Tiberius, we also have the time frame set for Chapter 12. Tiberius reigned from AD 14 to 37. "At that time," or, as the Hebrew order is, "And at time that shall stand up..." is the introduction of Michael. He is here called the great prince, but as we saw in our previous study, he is Jesus Christ Himself. With this ending of Chapters 10 and 11, we have achieved full harmony to Chapter 12 without making the slightest disruption of the scripture.

Daniel: Chapter 8

Now the time has come for Chapter 8. This chapter is a mystic chapter. One reason is because it has been unclear when the end of the 2,300 evenings and mornings were to be finished and what the meaning might be. Another reason is the description about a wicked king, a master of intrigue, who has been hard to figure out. Many have studied this part of Daniel without coming to a convincing conclusion. Since we already have studied Chapters 9–12, we have a solid base, full of harmony to stand on. Let us therefore go right in to Chapter 8 and start with verse 1:

> *"In the third year of King Belshazzar's reign, I, Daniel had a **vision**, after the one that had already appeared to me."*

This is correct. It is Daniel's second vision. Daniel saw one vision and received an explanation of it in Chapter 7. These visions in Chapter 2 and 4 were not originally Daniel's, but he was the human deliverer of the explanation in Nebuchadnezzar's visions. We also know that this king, Belshazzar, was king over Babylon and this vision came two years after Daniel's first vision. In verses 2–4 we read:

> *"In my vision I saw myself in the citadel of Susa in the province of Elam; in the vision I was beside the Ulai Canal. I looked up, and there before me was a **ram with two horns**, standing beside the canal, and the horns were long. One of the horns was longer than the other but grew up later. I watched the ram as he charged toward the west and the north and the south. No animal could stand against him, and none could rescue from his power. He did as he pleased and became great."*

In verse 20 of the same chapter we have the well known interpretation, given by the angel Gabriel:

> *"The two-horned ram that you saw represents the kings of **Media and Persia**."*

The Bible is here so clear that it explains itself. This fits also very well into the other visions showing the same world order. The animal has two horns, suiting the two parts of this Empire. We have both the Medes and the Persians. As you saw, one of the horns came up later, which is the Persian part. These world kingdoms are well known to everyone studying history. In verse 4 we can read how this kingdom expanded in all the directions mentioned, toward the west, north and south. No other kingdom could match this kingdom. Babylon's power was gone, and it was too early for the next world kingdom to rise. The Medes and the Persians did as they pleased. Let us continue with verses 5–8:

> *"As I was thinking about this, suddenly a **goat** with a **prominent horn** between his eyes came from the west, crossing the whole earth without touching the ground. He came toward the two-horned ram I had seen standing beside the canal and charged at him in great rage. I saw him attack the ram furiously, striking the ram and shattering his two horns. The ram was powerless to stand against him; the goat knocked him to the ground and trampled on him, and none could rescue the ram from his power. The goat became very great, but at the height of his power his large horn was broken off, and **in its place four prominent horns** grew up towards the four winds of heaven."*

In verses 21–22 the angel continues to give the interpretation.

> *"The shaggy goat is the king of **Greece**, and the large horn between his eyes is the first king. The four horns that replaced the one that was broken off represent **four kingdoms that will emerge from his nation** but will not have the same power."*

As always in world history, it is hard to stay on top

militarily for a very long time. For one reason or another, the power is eventually subsiding and making room for another kingdom. Greece was the third world nation after Babylon and Media Persia and was rising to be a very powerful kingdom. Again there is no question about the truth of this interpretation, since the Bible itself gives us the clue. The first big and prominent king of Greece was Alexander the Great. He conquered the known world so fast that it seemed he was not even touching the ground. Alexander the Great was very young, only thirty-three. He died a tragic death due to overconsumption of alcohol. This happened because he thought he was invincible. Yes, he had been extremely successful in the battlefield but his body was the same as ours. In his pride he wanted to show that he could drink plenty of alcohol without being harmed. This was not the case, and he died. This is the same type of pride which happened to King Nebuchadnezzar in Babylon. You will read about that later on. When Alexander the Great died, his four generals took over his kingdom and split it into four pieces. But as the angel tells us, they never became as powerful as Greece under Alexander the Great. So far, most historians agree without any arguments. From now on, however, we need to be very careful in our study. In the last part of verse 8 and verse 22 we read that the four horns emerged from his nation Greece. Let us now add verses 9–11:

> *"Out of them came another horn, which started small but grew in power to the south and to the east and **toward the Beautiful Land**. It grew until it reached the host of the heavens, and it threw some of the starry host down to the earth and trampled on them. It set itself up to be **as great as the Prince of the host**; it **took away the daily sacrifice** from him, and the place of his sanctuary was brought low."*

Now comes another horn. It is coming from one of the mentioned four horns. This is a kingdom. It starts small but is growing in power. The directions of the power are also given. It is growing towards the south and the east and toward the Beautiful Land. If we now go to Chapter 7, we know that the fourth world power is the Roman empire. There we read that this power was "terrifying and frightening and very powerful. It had large iron teeth; it crushed and devoured its victims and trampled underfoot whatever was left. It was different from all the former beasts." This quotation is from Chapter 7 and verse 7. The consensus is that this empire in Chapter 7 is the Roman empire. In our previous study, we have also confirmed the connection to Chapters 10 to 12. In Chapter 11:16, we have the "invader" who will do as he pleases, and he also establishes himself in the Beautiful Land, which is Israel. In Chapter 2, which we will study in a later chapter, we also find the fourth world empire. In verse 40 we read: "Finally, there will be a fourth kingdom, strong as iron—for iron breaks and smashes everything to pieces, so it will crush and break all the others." In Chapter 2 we find what is called the fourth but also the last world power. After that no more world powers will emerge. Again, this is strongly supported to be the Roman empire. If we now go back to Chapter 8, we have the connection to Chapter 7 and the fourth beast when it comes trampling down and the connection to Chapter 12 when it comes to invading the Beautiful Land. The Roman occupation of Israel is well known to anyone studying the four gospels. No world power was so brutal, cruel, crushing people, etc., as the fourth beast or the Roman Empire.

Then, however, it says it "grew until it reached the host of heavens." What could that be? Can this be found anywhere in the other visions in Daniel? Can this still be an earthly power? In one way or another, the direction is different. It shows also an attitude of confrontation towards heaven. This confrontation cannot be meant literally. Even in our modern space age, we have not truly come close to reaching the host of heaven. We have expanded our territory to the moon, Mars and a few other planets in our own solar system. But that's it. What is meant here? In Chapter 2 there is no clue to find. In Chapter 7 there are similarities. Let us look at them carefully. In Daniel 7 and verse

23 we have the fourth beast defined and understood to be the Roman Empire. In verse 24 we then find the splitting up of the Roman Empire into 10 horns. As we will see, this is declared to be the European states. In Daniel 7:24 we read:

> *"The ten horns are ten kings who will come from this kingdom (the Roman empire).* **After them** *another king will arise, different from the earlier ones, he will subdue three kings."*

In Chapter 7 we first have the Roman Empire, then the 10 European states formed, and then a different king that will arise. He will speak against the Most High, oppress the saints, try to change set times and laws and so on. As you will see in some of the next chapters, this is understood not to be the secular Roman Empire but to be the papacy. If we now go back to Chapter 8:23 and read the angel's explanation, we might find some other clues:

> *"In the latter part of their reign, when rebels have become completely wicked, a stern-faced* **king,** *a* **master of intrigue,** *will arise."*

The time is here declared, and we find it to be "in the latter part of their reign." Their reign is the previous four kings after Alexander the Great's death. It is not coming sometime later. It is very definite. It says "in the latter part of their reign." That means it is the following world power after Greece. It is not following after the 10 European states, as we will see about the little horn in Chapter 7. The king in Chapter 8 is therefore best understood to be the Roman Empire. Let us now read the vision about this king in Chapter 8:10–12:

> *"It grew until it* **reached the host of the heavens,** *and it threw some of the* **starry host down to the earth and trampled on them.** *It set itself up to be* **as great as the Prince of the host;** *it* **took away the daily sacrifice** *from him, and the place of* **his sanctuary was brought low.** *Because of rebellion, the host of the saints and the daily sacrifice were*

*given over to it. It prospered in everything it did, and the **truth was thrown to the ground.**"*

We need to go through all these things mentioned above. The understanding of these sentences is very important. However, before we do this, we will read the explanation from the angel, from verse 24–25 so that we can get as broad a picture as possible of this king:

> *"He will become very **strong**, but **not by his own power**. He will cause astounding **devastation** and will succeed in whatever he does. He will **destroy the mighty** men and the **holy people**. He will cause deceit to prosper, and he will **consider himself superior**. When he feels secure, he will destroy many and **take his stand against the Prince of princes**. Yet he will be **destroyed**, but **not by human power**."*

For your own interest, please repeat the text from our previous study in Chapter 11:21–45! With these passages you get the whole picture. We have already understood that the horn in verse 9 of Chapter 8 is the secular Roman Empire. The king who fits best with this description is Tiberius. Of course he is a secular emperor, but if you consider the other studies we have done and will do, the issue is very often about the word "dominion." The earthly rulers have the power to rule their empire, but who is ultimately in charge? Who has dominion? In all these visions in the book of Daniel, this is the most important question. All the kings in Daniel have to be confronted with the Most High. Read, for example, about King Nebuchadnezzar, King Belshazzar, King Darius and so on. They all had to take a stand against the Lord of Lords and they all had to accept Him as ruler. But with the Roman empire and especially the Emperor Tiberius, it was different. This is spelled out many times. In verse 23 of Chapter 7, it says that the king will be "different from all the other kingdoms." The whole section about Tiberius in Chapter 11:21–45 shows the difference.

Here in Chapter 8 we understand why he is different. In verse 24 we read that "he will become very strong, but not by his own power." If this king is very strong, but not by his own power, what power can it be? It is impossible to be the power of God, since the king will do a lot of things against the Prince of princes, which is Jesus Christ Himself. A kingdom cannot be divided against itself, as Jesus told the crowd. No, the only possibility is that the devil has received full control over this king and his actions. Then we can understand why the king is "completely wicked," "a stern-faced king," "master of intrigue," "caused astounding devastation," "destroyed the mighty," "caused deceit to prosper," "consider himself superior," "take a stand against the Prince of princes," and try to be "as great as the Prince of the host." All these things and much more can only fit a person totally in the hands of the devil. With this we will continue to study and see in what way this king can be a spiritual threat or a physical threat to the kingdom of God. This kingdom of God can be about our God in heaven or be about the Messiah as he walks on this earth or both.

One of the characteristics mentioned above about the Emperor Tiberius was that he was a "master of intrigue." In Chapter 11, where the same emperor is described in detail, we also find the word "intrigue" as an attribute for him. You can find this in Chapter 11:21. Another phrase was that he will cause astounding devastation (8:24) and he will succeed in everything he does. In Daniel Chapter 11:36 it says that "he will be successful until the time of the wrath," and in Daniel 8:12 we read that "it prospered in everything it did." This shows that we are studying the same king.

What the stern-faced king has done so far is bad, but what is coming hereafter is even worse. In verse 11 we read the horn, or the king, set himself up "to be as great as the Prince of the host." In verse 25, where we have the interpretation, he takes his stand against the Prince of princes. This cannot be anyone but Jesus Christ. In Chapter 9 Jesus is described as the "Most Holy," "the Anointed

One" and "the Ruler." Besides these terms, Jesus is also the meaning behind the word "sanctuary." In Chapter 12 the name "Michael" is used for Jesus Christ. Here in Chapter 8 we find "Prince of host," "Prince of princes," and they are without hesitation meant to represent our Savior Jesus Christ. We also read about the mighty in verse 24. If we read the sentence again it will be: "He will destroy the mighty (men) and the holy people." In NIV the word "men" is added but is not in the Hebrew. That's why it is put in brackets above. In Strong's Dictionary of Bible words, this word "mighty" means powerful, great, strong. If the word "men" is taken away, this sentence fits very well on Jesus Christ. That gives harmony to several other expressions. Look, for instance, at verse 11 where it says that "his sanctuary was brought low" or that "the truth was thrown to the ground." In previous chapters we have understood that the sanctuary as well as the Truth are pictures of Jesus Christ. The same verse also mentions about "the daily sacrifice was taken away" and, in the next verse, 12, that the daily sacrifice was given over to it. All these expressions are strongly pointing towards the death of Jesus on the cross.

If we now start to look at the time of this, we can get even more support for the ministry of Jesus in this world and His dying on the cross. In verse 9 we saw before that this time fits very well with the fourth world beast, which is the Roman Empire. But let us now go to verse 19. Here the angel gives the time indications:

> "He said: 'I am going to tell you what will happen later in the time of **wrath**, because the vision concerns the **appointed time of the end**.' "

The first thought might be that this is an end time vision of this world, especially since the word "wrath" is used. The last sentence at first impression seems to support this with the words "time of the end." However, it is worth studying more in the Bible. In Luke, Chapter 21, Jesus is talking about the end of the temple function in Jerusalem and about His second coming. Let us read from verses 23–24:

> *"There will be great distress in the land and **wrath** against **this people**. They will fall by the sword and will be taken as prisoners to all the nations. Jerusalem will be **trampled** on by the Gentiles until the times of the Gentiles are fulfilled."*

In this text you find a lot of similarities. We know, according to the question to Jesus and according to the answer, that this is fulfilled by the Israelites. In their process of rejecting the Messiah, there will be great distress in their land. Spiritual war is going on, as we studied before. We have already understood this to be the time of Jesus' Ministry on this earth. Wrath is a punishment, and in this context it is severalfold but not least the separation from God as the chosen people. It is also fulfilled by falling by the sword and spreading of the Jewish people all over the world. In this process we also notice the mentioning of the Gentiles. They are coming on the scene as a part of the victory on the cross, as we have understood from our studies in Chapters 9–12. So it is very possible to use Jesus' own words about the wrath in Luke and use them to enhance our understanding of Daniel 8:19.

The last part of verse 19 in Chapter 8 of Daniel is even more specific. It says that the vision "concerns the appointed time of the end." End of what? In the Hebrew it would be "in the last end of the indignation." The word "indignation" means to "foam at the mouth," "to be enraged," "abhor," "abominable," "be angry," etc. The word "appointed" is quite weak in comparison to the words used in Strong's Concordance. We read both in Daniel Chapters 9 and 12 as well as in Luke 21 about a time of distress and a time of war. This could fit with this time of Jesus' ministry, $3^1/_2$ years on this earth. The word "abominable" is even more interesting. If we read the same sentence again with this word, you will find the following: "the vision concerns the abominable time of the end." In our study about the last verses in Chapters 9 and 12, we understood the word "abominable" to be about the adopting of the Gentiles, so this is the time of the end for the Israelites and the time of adopting the Gentiles besides the Jews. This interpretation fits right into the theme of this book to find Christ as the center of the prophecies but also is in wonderful harmony with Chapters 9 to 12.

When studying the time in this prophecy, we have to go to verse 13. There we have the compressed vision in only one verse. We read:

> *"Then I heard a holy one speaking, and another holy one said to him, 'How long will it take for the vision to be **fulfilled**?'"*

If you ask how long it will take, then you want to know the length of time. In the Hebrew it says: "Until when." With that question we are more interested in, up to what point in history is this vision fulfilled? You are focusing on the endpoint of this vision. By the way, what is the end-point? The rest of verse 13 is followed and explains what it is about:

> *"—the vision concerning the daily sacrifice, the rebellion that causes **desolation**, and the **surrender of the sanctuary** and of the **host** that will be **trampled** underfoot?"*

We remember the question to be "How long will it take for the vision to be **fulfilled**?" In other words, it is fulfilled when something happens to the daily sacrifice, when something causes desolation, when the sanctuary is surrendered and when the host is trampled underfoot. Is this a matter of one time where all these four things are fulfilled at the same time or is this a progressive row of events where the prophecy is fulfilled with the last part? Let us study them one by one.

DAILY SACRIFICE...

The daily (the true Hebrew translation) or the daily sacrifice, which most often is used, we find in verse 11 already. We do not need to speculate on what is going to happen to the daily. It is spelled out here:

*"It set itself up to be as great as the Prince of the host; it **took away** the daily sacrifice from him, and the place of his **sanctuary** was **brought low**,"*

Well, I am sure you already know the answer to this question. The daily sacrifice system was fulfilled when Jesus died on the cross (Daniel 9:27 and 12:11). When the Romans and the Israelites killed the Messiah, the sacrifice system was fulfilled and the curtain tore from top to bottom. The book of Hebrews tells us that Jesus once for all gave His life as a sacrifice. The blood on the cross is the fulfillment. With the death of the Lamb, the previous slaughter of animals came to be useless. With His death and His death alone, this part of the texts was fulfilled. It happened in 31 AD.

THE REBELLION THAT CAUSES DESOLATION...

When we studied Chapter 9, we saw in the prayer of Daniel how he confessed sins. He prayed there in verse 5 saying that "we have been wicked and we have rebelled; we have turned away from your commands and laws." In other words, they have sinned. The word "rebellion" is, however, more profound than to sin. The word "rebellion" has more of an active part of not choosing the right way. We are dealing more with opposition and rejection. This is exactly what we can read about in Matthew 22, in the parable of the wedding banquet. We have studied this earlier, but here Jesus tells us the consequences of the rejection of the Messiah. This rebellion will cause the divorce of God towards the Israelites and God will open the doors for anyone to come in to His banquet. God will therefore accept the spiritual Israel. The number two fulfillment of the vision is the divorce of the Israelites. According to Ephesians 2:11–22 we have seen that this divorce happened when Jesus died on the cross. Again, this happened in 31 AD.

TRAMPLING OF SANCTUARY AND HOST...

In John Chapter 2 we read before about the background to the understanding of the whole of Daniel's book.

Mistakes are made when taking a spiritual fulfillment to be a literal fulfillment. It is not wrong to see whether the temple building in Jerusalem has anything to do with the prophecy. But if you have no success with that philosophy, you can try some other routes of thinking. However, Jesus Himself tells us in the book of Revelation that "He is the Alpha and Omega," the starter and the finisher, in Revelation 1:8. If we take that seriously, we should start the study of a prophecy to check and see if anything in it has to do with Jesus Christ. Therefore, let's go back to Jesus' own statement in John 2:18–21. There we read:

> *"Then the Jews demanded of Him, 'What miraculous sign can you show us to prove your authority to do all this?' Jesus answered them, '**Destroy this temple, and I will raise it again in three days.**' The Jews replied, 'It has taken forty-six years to build this temple, and you are going to raise it in three days?' **But the temple He had spoken of was His body.**"*

This text is the basis for our interpretation of Daniel, and this text we need to take into consideration here as well. If the sanctuary was not meant to be the temple built of stones, it must have been meant to be the body of Jesus Himself. This is exactly what Jesus is saying in the last sentence. He is connecting the death of Himself with the destroying of the temple. "But the temple he had spoken of was his body." That gives us all the authority we need to see if Jesus is the fulfillment in Daniel 8.

Before we go on, we need to understand something else. What is the meaning of the word "surrender"? If we look this up, the word "trampled" is actually used. The word "trampled" we find both in Hebrew and in KJV. Then the sentence is about "the trampling of the sanctuary and the host." That is the sentence that we need to understand. The word "trampling" is quite clear in itself. Another way of expressing this could be "to tread upon" or "oppress." In Hebrew 10:10, 19–20 as well as 28–29, we read:

*"And by that will, we have been made holy through the **sacrifice of the body of Jesus Christ** once for all."*

*"Therefore, brothers, since we have confidence to enter the Most Holy Place **by the blood of Jesus**, by a new living way opened for us through the **curtain, that is his body**,"*

*"Anyone who rejected the law of Moses died without mercy on the testimony of two or three witnesses. How much more severely do you think a man deserves to be punished who has **trampled the Son of God under foot**, who has treated as an unholy thing the **blood of the covenant** that sanctified him, and who has insulted the Spirit of grace?"*

We know that when Jesus died on the cross, He died for us personally once for all. The curtain in the temple tore and we have through His blood access to the almighty God. We are one with Him. The reason for this is that He was treated in the same manner that we should have been treated. We deserve to be trampled on, but Jesus is the one who was trampled. We understood above that the word "trampled" also means "oppressed." In Isaiah Chapter 53:7–8 we read this well-known passage:

*"He was **oppressed** and afflicted, yet He did not open His mouth; He was led like a lamb to the slaughter, and as a sheep before her shearers is silent, so He did not open His mouth. By **oppression** and judgment He was taken away. And who can speak of His descendants? For He was **cut off from the living**; for the transgression of my people He was stricken."*

If we combine this sentence that Jesus was trampled on with the previous sentence, like "his sanctuary was brought low," "truth was thrown to the ground," it gives us overwhelming support that all these expressions are about Jesus, especially since the word "truth" is the same as "faithful" and "trustworthiness." With all the cruelty and affliction He experienced, He was surely oppressed and trampled on especially when He died on the cross. This statement in the vision is also fulfilled on the cross. This event took place in 31 AD as we all know.

TRAMPLING OF THE HOST...

When we come to this expression, we find that the trampling of the sanctuary is connected to the trampling of the host. In verse 12 we see that the daily sacrifice and the "host of the saints were given over to it." Finally in verse 13 we read about the trampling of the sanctuary and the host. These examples are all from the vision. If we now turn to the interpretation, we find in verse 24 the following statement:

*"He will destroy the mighty and the **holy people**."*

In our previous studies we found that both the words "sanctuary" and "mighty" are the same as Jesus Christ. From verse 13 we understand that the trampling of Christ and subsequently the trampling of the host will take place and be fulfilled after 2,300 evenings and mornings. The trampling of the host will obviously end on the cross. In this context, the host connected to Jesus Christ must be the true believers of God. It is not explained in these verses who the host is. The only decision we can make so far is that they are the children of God.

However, in verse 10 we read about "the starry host," which was thrown down to earth and trampled on. This starry host might be different than the host described above. When reading this text, the thoughts are going to Revelation Chapter 12:3–4, where it says:

*"an enormous red dragon with seven heads and ten horns and seven crowns on his head. His tail **swept a third of the stars** out of the sky and flung them **to the earth**."*

Later on in verse 9 we read that the dragon and his angels were hurled down to the earth. With that in mind, we need to know that when Satan fell into sin once upon a time, he convinced one third of the angels to be on his side. These holy beings decided to go from the light to the darkness. When Satan was defeated by Christ on the cross, not only the devil but also all the fallen angels were suffering the same judgment. The devil is then responsible for the angels being hurled down to this earth and trampled on. With this understanding, the fallen angels got their sentence at the same time as the devil. This interpretation could be the understanding of the word "host" in Daniel Chapter 8 and was therefore fulfilled in AD 31 when Jesus died on the cross.

The most likely interpretation, however, is that the "host" in verse 13 which, in the explanation in verse 24, is called "the holy people," has the same meaning as in Chapters 9 and 12. In Chapter 9 it says that seventy "sevens" are decreed for "your people and your holy city," and in Chapter 12 it talks about when the power of "the holy people" finally has been broken. In these two passages we have already decided the meaning to be God's chosen people, the Israelites, and their shortcoming as a nation. Their time as God's chosen nation was finished AD 31.

Now it is time to go back to the question in Daniel Chapter 8:13. We see a holy one talking to another holy being. The question we read in that verse is: "How long will it take for the vision to be fulfilled?" The vision is then defined to be about: (1) When the daily sacrifice was taken away. (2) When the rebellion that caused desolation was fulfilled. (3) When Christ was trampled on (4) When the host was trampled on. All these events were fulfilled at the death of Jesus Christ on the cross. Since the time is asked for, the answer is 31 AD. Thus the vision in Chapter 8 was fulfilled at this time in history. The next question is, "How will this understanding now fit to the 2,300 evenings and mornings?"

2,300 EVENINGS AND MORNINGS...

Now we have come to the final verses in Daniel Chapter 8. This must fit the answer to the question above. If this explanation of the vision and the interpretation of the vision is in harmony with the rest of Daniel Chapter 8 and also with Chapters 9–12, we are standing on safe ground. In our studies so far, we have been able to understand that Chapters 9–12 are dealing with Christ's ministry on this earth and the consequences of His life and death here. We have also seen that in Chapter 8, the prophecy can very easily be fulfilled in Jesus. If that is the case, we should also be able to find Jesus Christ in the last verses of Chapter 8. Let us read the final statement in the vision in verse 14 and then read the interpretation in verse 26:

*"He said to me, 'It will take **2,300** evenings and mornings; then the **sanctuary will be reconsecrated**.'"*

*"**The vision** of the evenings and mornings that has been given you **is true**, but seal up the vision, for it concerns the distant future."*

In Daniel's vision, he hears two angels talking to each other. One asks when the vision is going to be fulfilled. Even if the vision were described in the earlier verses, from verse 9–12, the angel repeats the content of the vision one more time in verse 13. This verse is short and hardly gives any new information. This repetition is there for our sake. We need to understand the question and know what the answer is focused on. The answer is concentrated on the fulfillment of the prophecy. The answer is, of course, intimately related to the question, which is the center of this prophecy. The content of the vision, we numbered from 1 to 4 and analyzed it in detail above. If you ask how long a time it will take until it is fulfilled, you need a starting point to come to the endpoint. But it is also possible to know the endpoint and then calculate backwards and come to the starting point.

If we now look at the length of the prophecy, we read about 2,300 evenings and mornings. This is quite an unusual description. Most often we would find it expressed in days, weeks, months and years and so on. Here evenings and mornings are used. If we look into this we have actually four options. One option is to take it literally. If so, we can have 2,300 days. Since evenings and mornings are used, it is also correct to split this number in two. Every day has both one evening and one morning. That makes two of this kind per day and the total will be 1,150 days. You can find this concept in Genesis during the creation of the world. In Genesis 1 and verse 5 we read:

> *"And there was **evening** and there was **morning**—the **first day**."*

This sentence with evenings and mornings is repeated after every creation day. And every 24-hour day was of this kind. The word "evening" is used first, the same as in Daniel 8 in connection with the 2,300 evenings and mornings. You can also use this time in a prophetic way and say that one day equals one year. With this option there could either be 2,300 years or 1,150 years. It is up to the reader and the guidance of the Holy Spirit to decide what is appropriate to use. After studying some other aspects, we will return with a final determination in regard to this issue.

SANCTUARY...

The next word in Daniel 8:13 after the time interval to be used is "the sanctuary." Of course this can always be used literally, and then you have to come to an understanding of when the temple building with stone and other materials will be reconsecrated. If something is reconsecrated, it must have been made unholy before. With this concept, many have the destruction of the temple in 70 AD as a start and then look into the future to find some event where the temple could be reconsecrated again. So far there is no good Biblical explanation for this reconsecration. The other option is to continue to use the word "sanctuary" as Jesus did. We read it earlier in John Chapter 2:18–21. In that passage, Jesus uses the word "temple" when He is talking about His body. With this book's concept, there will be 2,300 evenings and mornings until something happens to the sanctuary, meaning the body of Jesus.

RECONSECRATED...

The next concept to understand is what will happen to the body of Jesus. In NIV it says that it will be reconsecrated. Again, if it is reconsecrated, it must have been broken down, destroyed before or been trampled down earlier. Otherwise, it cannot be reconsecrated. We have seen this in Chapter 8, and there are several examples of it. We read above about "the trampled sanctuary," "the sanctuary was brought low," etc. With the life and death of Jesus Christ here on this earth, this oppression of Christ took place. In Isaiah Chapter 53:7–8, we again read how this took place:

> "He was **oppressed** and afflicted, yet He did not open His mouth; He was led like a lamb to the slaughter, and as a sheep before her shearers is silent, so He did not open His mouth. By **oppression** and judgment He was taken away. And who can speak of His descendants? For He was **cut off from the living**; for the transgression of my people He was stricken."

If you look at this verse, when was Jesus oppressed and afflicted? In the first sentence, you can see that He was oppressed and afflicted when He still was alive. The whole ministry of Jesus was pointing towards His dying on the cross. He was the only one who was carrying all the sins of the world. Jesus suffered all the pain we should have suffered. He took on Himself all our afflictions. So there is no doubt that Jesus was oppressed and trampled on. But when was, then, Jesus reconsecrated? If we look up synonym words to the Hebrew word for reconsecrated, we find expressions like "to be right," "to make right" (in a moral or forensic sense), "cleanse," "clear self," "be just," "do just," "be righteous," "turn to righteousness," "vindicated." Jesus was oppressed and afflicted all His life but especially the last days and hours of His life. When was the sanctuary cleansed? When was everything made right in a moral and forensic sense? When was unrighteousness turned to righteousness? At what time in history were unholy things made just? When did the vindication take place? All these words and sentences with these words point toward one event. When the Messiah died on the cross, the victory was accomplished; everything was done. The last words of Jesus, just before taking His last breath, were "It is done." Because of this victory, He would rise from the dead a couple of days later. This resurrection is wonderful but was possible only through His victory in the death on the cross.

We read earlier from Revelation 12:7–12 about the war in heaven. Michael, Jesus Christ, and His angels were involved in a war in heaven. The war was against the devil and his angels. We read about the victory in heaven and the devil and his angels were hurled down to this earth. The victory in heaven took place, and the reason we find in verse 11:

> "They overcame him by the **blood of the Lamb.**"

By the blood of Jesus, the victory was won over all the evil forces in the whole universe. But this is not the only effect of the blood of the Lamb. In Revelation 7:14 we read that:

> "They have washed their robes and made them white in the **blood of the Lamb.**"

Romans 5:9 says:

> "Since we now have been **justified by his blood,** how much more shall we be saved from God's wrath through him!"

Matthew 26:28 says:

> "This is **my blood of the covenant,** which is poured out for many for the forgiveness of sins."

With all these texts we can see that the blood of Jesus, shed on the cross, is the act to salvation, the forgiveness of sins and the reason for eternal redemption. With the death on the cross, we are made just, we are made righteous, we are cleansed. Why? Because Jesus bore all our sins and they were nailed on the cross. When Christ took our sins, He was made to sin. He had lived a sinless life, but He was made to be a sinner. This is a part of the trampling on Jesus. But with His victory, He not only saved us and cleansed us of all our sins, He Himself was cleansed of all our sin. This cleansing of all our sins on Him is the cleansing of the sanctuary. With this act we can understand what Hebrew 9:12 means for us:

> *"But he entered the Most Holy Place once for all by his own blood, having obtained **eternal redemption.**"*

With this act the whole sacrificial system in the temple should have been brought to an end. Everything was accomplished. Everything was done. Nothing can be added to it. We can either accept it or not. Taking all these verses into consideration, verse 14 in Daniel 8 could be read as follows: "It will take 2,300 evenings and mornings; then the body of Jesus will be cleansed from the sin of the world." Isn't this a wonderful sentence! We are cleansed from all our sins and Jesus is cleansed, carrying our sin. This interpretation makes perfect sense in regard to our studies so far in Chapters 8 to 12 in the book of Daniel. In 31 AD all these things happened. What is, then, the meaning of the 2,300 evenings and mornings?

THE MEANING OF THE 2,300 EVENINGS AND MORNINGS...

The initial question was; "How long will it take for the vision to be fulfilled?" The question is a time span. The time span in itself is not the importance or the fulfillment, but during this time it continues to happen until it is fulfilled. We understood before that the devil is behind the Roman Empire and the Emperor Tiberius in a very special way. We also know that the devil is attacking Jesus in the best and smartest ways he ever could devise. Very early in the ministry of Jesus, actually right after the baptism of Jesus, we find the tremendous temptations of Jesus. In Matthew 4 we can read about Jesus fasting for 40 days and 40 nights. In the severe hunger, the devil challenged Him to make bread of the stones if Jesus is the Son of God. What a horrendous temptation! The second temptation is again challenging Jesus to be the Son of God. The third temptation, however, was different. It was about dominion. In Matthew 4:8–9 we read that:

> *"the devil took Jesus up to a very high mountain and showed Him all the kingdoms of the world and their splendor. 'All this will I give you,' he (the devil) said 'if you will bow down and worship me.'"*

Jesus did not fall. He was victorious. Here the devil set himself "up to be as great as the Prince of the host," as it is read in Daniel 8:11. But, really "all the kingdoms of the world"? Yes, the devil is the prince of this world, and all this could have been Jesus' if He had bowed down. However, Jesus also knew that all this and much more would belong to Him if He continued to be faithful to His Father in heaven. These temptations were just at the beginning of Jesus' ministry, and the devil set himself up to be as great as the Son of Man. This is the range of the fulfillment of the prophecy, from the very first part of Jesus' ministry to His death on the cross.

How long will it take for the vision to be fulfilled was the question. It will take 2,300 evenings and mornings, which is the same as 1,150 days. Then the fulfillment of this prophecy will take place. Then the death on the cross will take place. The ministry of Jesus lasted about 3 and a half years according to Daniel Chapter 9. As we saw earlier, this time span of 3 and a half years is not a very accurate length. But in Daniel 8 we are dealing with a very determined time span. If we do a calculation, 2,300 evenings and mornings is the same as 1,150 days, which is the same as 3 years, 2 months and 10 days. What we can see is that this time span is shorter than 3 and a half years.

On the other hand, we understood the time span from AD 31, the death of Jesus, to AD 34 to be somewhat more than 3 and a half years. If we add these two time periods together, we will almost get the full seven years. Can this be acceptable? In a time prophecy of 490 years, as in Daniel Chapter 9, this time accuracy is more than acceptable. We are happy to know the year when Artaxerxes gave the order to build up Jerusalem. We do not know what day or month the decree came from this emperor. Thus a couple of months is not a problem for this long prophecy covering a time of 490 years. However, 2,300 evenings and mornings or 1,150 days is a very accurate time period. Is there any historical evidence of Jesus' time in ministry on this earth? Do we know exactly when He got baptized and exactly what day He was crucified?

HISTORICAL EVIDENCES ABOUT THE TIME OF JESUS' MINISTRY…

Under this title, we are going to find out when the ministry of Jesus started and when it was ended on the cross. It seems to be hard to find proof of evidence, but there are several indications about this time period. The ministry of this book is to get the information from the Bible alone and not go to any other sources. This does not mean that sources outside the Bible are incorrect. But the Bible has so much information in itself that it is a challenge and a joy to find everything needed in the Bible. What we need is to find a passage in the Bible which tells us when the ministry of Jesus started. By the way, what can be understood by the word "ministry?" In Webster we find the definition "period of service." In the case of Jesus, service has to do with the very reason He came to this earth. This reason is to present Himself to the public and to show that He is the "way" to salvation, to show that He is the Son of God and to redeem the world. If we look at the gospels we can find this in Matthew. Let us start to read in Chapter 3:16–17:

*"As soon as **Jesus was baptized**, he went up out of*

*the water. At that moment heaven was opened, and he saw the **Spirit of God descending like a dove** and lighting on him. And a voice from heaven said, '**This is my Son**, whom I love; with him I am well pleased.'"*

What a special moment! Imagine being there when this happened. This was the moment when Jesus received the power and wisdom needed to do His ministry. This was given to Him as the Spirit of God. But it does not say here that from this moment the ministry was started. After the baptism Jesus did not start to preach, heal, and comfort the people around Him. The baptism was, however, absolutely necessary for the ministry, but the beginning came later on. The next verse in Matthew Chapter 4:1 tells us that Jesus was led into the desert. There He fasted for 40 days and 40 nights. After the fasting, the devil came with his temptations. We have already studied those temptations, and Jesus passed these tremendously difficult but important tests. In verse 11 the devil is leaving Jesus and the angels attended Him. 40 days after His baptism have passed, and still the starting point has not been given. In verse 12, Jesus hears the bad news about John the Baptist. He has been put in prison. This must have been another hard stress and temptation for Jesus Christ. At this moment the prophecy was not yet fulfilled to start His ministry. In verses 12–16 we read:

*"When Jesus heard that John had been put in prison, he **returned to Galilee**. Leaving Nazareth, he went and **lived in Capernaum**, which was by the lake in the area of Zebulon and Naphtali—to fulfill what was said through the prophet Isaiah: 'Land of Zebulon and land of Naphtali, the way to the sea, along the Jordan, Galilee of the Gentiles—the people living in darkness have seen a great light; on those living in the land of the shadow of death a light has dawned.' "*

The last part of these verses in Matthew is a quotation from Isaiah; and in Chapter 9:1–2, we find this quotation. Just a few verses later in Isaiah 9, we find these wonderful verses about the Messiah. This passage ends with the following well-known words in verse 6:

> *"For to us a child is born, to us a son is given, and the government will be on his shoulders. And he will be called **Wonderful Counselor, Mighty God, Everlasting Father, Prince of Peace.**"*

Matthew, writing the gospel, realizes that Jesus, according to the prophecy in Isaiah, had to move from Nazareth and live in Capernaum. Since Capernaum is in the Land of Zebulon and of Naphtali by the lake called Sea of Galilee, Jesus had to live there for a while. That is why it says he went there and lived there. How long a time He lived in Capernaum we do not know. In KJV it says that Jesus "dwelt" in Capernaum. To be able to dwell there He had to move there. After that was fulfilled we read in Matthew 4:17:

> *"From **that time** on **Jesus began to preach**, "Repent, for the kingdom of heaven is near."*

In the Greek it says: "From then began Jesus to proclaim and to say…" This is what we are looking for. This is the starting point of Jesus' Ministry. The Bible itself tells us when the Ministry starts. It did not start with the baptism nor with the temptations from the devil. Jesus had to withdraw to Nazareth first and then move to Capernaum to fulfill the prophecy. After that, the ministry of Jesus on this earth was started and He went among the people.

Now to the connection to the 2,300 evenings and mornings, which we understood to be 1,150 days. The last week or last seven years of the 490-year prophecy in Daniel 9 lasts from 27 AD to 34 AD. A seven-year time is a total of 2,520 days. According to our study in Daniel Chapter 12, there will be 1,290 days from the death on the cross to the stoning of Stephen. If we take the total amount of days in this last week and subtract 1,290 days, we have only 1,230 days left. 2,520 days—1,290 days=1,230 days. Consequently, there is a total of 1,230 days from the baptism of Jesus to His crucifixion. If Jesus went straight to the fasting in the desert after His baptism, we have another 40 days which we have to subtract. 1,230–40 = 1,190 days. After the fasting period we have the temptations. But we do not know how long a time they took. After the temptations we know the angels attended Jesus. After a fasting period of 40 days, you may need a couple days to recuperate. In another translation it says that the angels cared for Jesus. The next thing to happen was the return to Nazareth in Galilee. This He did after hearing about the imprisonment of John the Baptist. Jesus withdrew to Nazareth, as another translation tells us. How long He stayed in Nazareth, we do not know. Thereafter Jesus moved to Capernaum and lived there. Is it possible to do these things in 40 days? This is the time we have left to use to come to 1,150 days. So if we summarize:

1) Breaking the fast and being attended by the angels.

2) Thereafter Jesus withdrew to Nazareth in Galilee after hearing about John the Baptist being put in prison.

3) Move to Capernaum and "live" there to fulfill the prophecy from Isaiah Chapter 9 according to Matthew 4:13–14.

These events could take place in more or less than 40 days. Since we never will be able to prove the time of these events, we have to accept it by faith. According to the prophecy, this is the time needed to be fulfilled. Let us summarize this with a diagram:

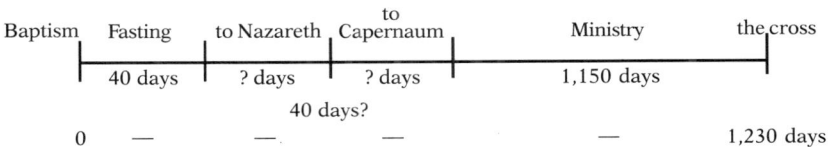

Baptism	Fasting	to Nazareth	to Capernaum	Ministry	the cross
	40 days	? days	? days	1,150 days	
		40 days?			
0	—	—	—	—	1,230 days

This diagram is not there to prove but to show how reasonable this time schedule is. If this appears reasonable to you and you are willing to accept this in faith, the 2,300 evenings and mornings or 1,150 days is a very firm fact and fits right into the prophecy in Daniel Chapter 8 as well as the whole book of Daniel. If the historical experts can give us more support about these dates, that is fine. But even without their support, the Bible gives us just the right information to understand and trust the prophecy by faith.

COMPARISON OF THE VISIONS...

It has been fascinating to see the closeness of the three visions in Chapters 8–12. They all seem to comment on the same subject, about Jesus Christ Himself. They are all pointing out the ministry of the Messiah. If we look at the time aspect, we find that Chapter 8 is dealing with the first part of the seven years. Chapter 9 is describing the whole week, which is the same as the seven years. Chapters 10–12 are dealing with the time from the cross and the last part of these seven years. Chapter 8 deals with Christ's affliction, suffering and taking on all the sins of this world on His shoulders. Chapter 9 deals with the promise of the Messiah and the "cutting off" of the Anointed One. Chapters 10–12 are talking about the consequences of the death of the Messiah, for example, that the power of the holy people will be broken and the Gentiles will be accepted.

CHAPTER 8	CHAPTER 9	CHAPTERS 10–12
First part of the 7 years	The seven years	The last part of the 7 years
40+40+1,150= 1,230 days	7 years or 2,520 days	1,290 days
Vision + Interpretation	Prayer + Interpretation	Vision + Interpretation
Vision sealed to the end time	Vision not sealed	Vision sealed to the end time
Time for Israelites to atone	Jesus divorces the Israelites	Gentiles and Israelites are accepted
The trampling on Jesus	The dying of Jesus	The consequences of His death
Jesus carries the sins	The atonement for sin	Promise of everlasting life

With this study so far we have looked at the first coming of Jesus in a prophetic way. The differences and the similarities have been pointed out. The very essence of the ministry of Jesus has been proclaimed. The atonement for all sins has been made. The Gentiles and the Israelites are, since the cross of Christ, adopted by grace. All prophecies have been fulfilled, and God has been trustworthy to the covenant. God has turned around the failure of the Israelites as a nation and made it a worldwide success, the Jews included. In Romans, Paul is talking about the Israelites versus the Gentiles. Through what has happened on the cross, God has brought full blessing to both campuses. No one has the first place, since both are equal. No one can boast over the other. No one has a better chance than the other. No one has an indefinite assurance. The center is the root, and that is Jesus Christ and not the branches. To really see what all this has accomplished, let us read some verses from Romans Chapter 11.

11   "...because of their transgression, salvation has come to the Gentiles to make Israel envious."

12   "But if their transgression means riches for the world,
       and their loss means riches for the Gentiles, how
       much greater riches will their fullness bring!"

15   "For if their rejection is the reconciliation of the world,
       what will their acceptance be but life from death."

18   "do not boast over those branches. If you do, con-
       sider this: You do not support the root, but the root
       supports you."

21   "For if God did not spare the natural branches, he
       will not spare you either."

24   "After all, if you were cut out of an olive tree that is
       wild by nature, and contrary to nature were grafted
       into a cultivated olive tree, how much more readily
       will these, the natural branches, be grafted into their
       own olive tree!"

With this we have completed the study on the prophecies of the end time of the Israelites and the adoption by
grace for both the Israelites and the Gentiles. With this
all the people of the world are united into one body, the
body of Jesus Christ. This is the whole concept of the first
coming of Jesus. God wants us to be one in Christ as He is
one with His Father. Listen closely! If we for some reason
cannot be one with a believer of God regardless of denomination, we ourselves are consequently not one with
the Lord. We often tend to accuse someone else and not
ourselves if something is wrong in a relationship. But remember, since no one has a priority relationship towards
God, we can only blame ourselves if we experience fail-
ures in our spiritual relationships with our neighbors.
Christ has done His part, and He hopes we will do our
part. Let us condemn no one regardless of their belief system but love everyone as Jesus did on this earth. If so, you
are one with Christ and the Father and you can look forward with joy to the second coming of Jesus.

DUAL APPLICATION...

When it comes to Bible texts and prophecy, there are often many lessons to learn. If one pearl is found, still further insight can be gained. The Bible is so deep in wisdom and power that we never shall be tempted to believe that "this is it!" We must be open and flexible under the guidance of the Holy Spirit. The interpretations given in this book do concentrate on the spiritual fulfillment of the temple but in no way exclude dual application or many applications, like fulfillment on behalf of the literal temple. As a matter of fact, the purpose of this book is to widen the perspective of the understanding of the Bible. God alone has the total knowledge. Hopefully this book has so far been a positive challenge to you and inspired you to further studies.

Some readers may look at the literal fulfillment of the prophecy in regard to the temple. Your thoughts are concentrating on Jesus' speech in Matthew 24, Mark 13 and Luke 21 concerning the signs of the end. What is the connection to Daniel Chapters 8 to 12 and when should it be compared? To understand Jesus' speech we need to look at the background. Jesus and His disciples are leaving the temple in Jerusalem and the disciples are amazed at the buildings. In Mark 13:1–4 we read:

> "As he was **leaving the temple**, one of his disciples said to him, 'Look, Teacher! What massive stones! What magnificent buildings!' 'Do you see all these great buildings?' replied Jesus. '**Not one stone here will be left on another**; every one will be thrown down.' As Jesus was sitting on the Mount of Olives opposite the temple, Peter, James, John and Andrew asked him privately, 'Tell us **when** will these things happen? And what will be the **sign** that they are all **about to be fulfilled?**'"

From this conversation, which you can read in Matthew 24:1–3 and Luke 21:5–7 as well, they all talk about the literal fulfillment about the temple. The disciples are, in Mark Chapter 13, amazed at the beautiful buildings made of stone and timber. No one here talks about the temple as the body of Jesus Christ, which we studied in John 2:19–21. We can also see that Jesus' answer is dealing with the same issue when He states that "not one stone will be left on another." Of course, Jesus is making this clear on purpose. The question to Jesus is twofold: First, when it will happen and, secondly, what will the sign be? In other words, when will not one stone be left on another and what will be the sign just before the destruction of the temple building in Jerusalem? Is Jesus answering these two questions? We can read the answers in Mark 13:14:

> *"**When** you see 'the **abomination that causes desolation**' standing where it does not belong—let the reader understand—then let those who are in Judea flee to the mountains."*

In Luke 21:20 the abomination that causes desolation is further explained.

> *"**When** you see **Jerusalem being surrounded by armies**, you will know that its **desolation is near.**"*

With this text in Luke about the surrounding of the armies, in this case the Romans, the answer to both the questions "when" and "what sign" is the literal fulfillment of the prophecy of the temple. In all three gospels Jesus answers the question in the same way, even if Luke is more specific in this context. The Romans did destroy the temple and most of the city of Jerusalem, and not one stone was left on another. The temple was also desecrated at the same time. This is an exact fulfillment of Jesus' own prophecy about the temple building made of stones. In Matthew 24 Jesus makes a connection to the prophecies in Daniel Chapters 8–12, which makes this a dual application. Remember that the initial question was about the temple built of stones. The answer to the question "when," we afterwards know that it was fulfilled in AD 70. But for those living in that time, the "sign," the surrounding of Jerusalem by the Roman armies, was much more important. The Christian Jews who knew about this prophecy of

Jesus had, through this knowledge, a true chance and used it to flee to the mountains and be saved. To everyone who listened and kept His word, it could lead to a blessing and life.

What makes Matthew 24, Mark 13 and Luke 21 so challenging is that signs of the destruction of Jerusalem are mixed with signs about the second coming of Jesus. We are encouraged to use as much from these chapters as possible for our studies to understand the time before Jesus' second coming. However, always keep in mind that the initial question from the disciples was about the temple built of stones.

ANTICHRIST...

Antichrist can be defined in several ways and in general it can be said about anything pointing away from Jesus Christ instead of towards Him. For example, in the New Testament we find Jesus' teaching about salvation by grace, and through Him that is the only way of salvation. No one will be saved for the kingdom of God other than through Jesus Christ. Antichrist is, for example, salvation by works since it is promoting another way to salvation without Jesus Christ. According to that theory you will come to heaven if you are "good enough." Let us take another example. The Bible is the highest authority we as Christians believe in. Jesus says that He is the "Word" and the "Truth" and anything claimed to have higher authority than the Bible is also antichrist. Let us now read some texts about this. We read in 1 John 4:2–3 and 2 John 1:7:

> *"This is how you can **recognize the Spirit of God**: Every Spirit that acknowledges **that Jesus Christ has come** in the flesh **is from God**, but every spirit that **does not acknowledge Jesus** is not from God. This is the **spirit of antichrist**, which you have heard is coming and even now is already in the world."*

and in 2 John 1:7 it says:

*"Many deceivers, who **do not acknowledge Jesus Christ** as coming in the flesh, have gone out into the world. Any such person is the deceiver and the **antichrist.**"*

The understanding of antichrist is now hopefully clear. When it comes to the Book of Daniel there is something more that needs to be added. In our study so far, we have defined the words "sanctuary" or "temple" to be Jesus Christ Himself. This has given us a deeper understanding of the Book of Daniel as well as a timely fulfillment of the prophecies mentioned here. If we now move about 2,000 years forward in history and come to our time, we need to understand the following:

In our time many Christians as well as Jews are waiting for Israel to respond spiritually to the Messiah. This we all hope and pray for. However, some are also waiting for the Jews to again be the chosen people of God. This does not stand on firm Biblical ground. Others have never realized that the status was changed at the cross and still today believe the Jewish people to have a special meaning when it comes to the issue of salvation. This is sad since it is unbiblical, as you have seen in our previous study.

Furthermore, some believe that the temple in Jerusalem needs to be rebuilt again before the second coming of Jesus to fulfill some prophecy. If the temple ground in Jerusalem comes into Jewish dominion and if the temple is rebuilt as a historical museum, that would be very interesting for everyone. Many would love to go there and get a feel for the past history. One fear, however, would be that the temple again would regain some original status and in that aspect compete with the real temple, which is Jesus Christ. This temple building and the use of it could potentially be very misleading for the Jews, the Christians, and for people in other belief systems. If this would happen, the temple could easily be an antichrist as well. Remember, Christ dying on the cross is the only sacrifice needed and the "temple" is Jesus Christ Himself.

Daniel: Chapter 2

In the second year of Nebuchadnezzar's reign he had dreams that troubled his mind. He could not sleep. "Dreams," in plural, probably indicate that this situation was going on for some time. That's why he was troubled and could not sleep. The problem, however, was that Nebuchadnezzar himself could not remember the dream well enough to tell it; and without telling it to the wise men of his country, no human mind could interpret the dream either. As you may know, the king became furious and gave orders to kill all the wise men of Babylon. When Daniel discovered why he and his three friends were to be killed, Daniel asked for an audience with the king. Expecting God's intervention, Daniel requested some more time and, surprisingly, he got it because earlier the other wise men of Babylon tried to gain time but were not successful. In verse 17–18 we read:

> *"Then **Daniel** returned to his house and explained the matter to his friends Hananiah, Mishael and Azariah. He **urged them to plead for mercy from the God of heaven** concerning this mystery."*

During the night the mystery was revealed to Daniel in a vision. Then Daniel praised the God of heaven and had a wonderful prayer in verses 20–23:

> *"**Praise** be to the name of God for ever and ever; **wisdom and power are His.** He changes times and seasons; He sets up kings and deposes them. He gives wisdom to the wise and knowledge to the discerning. He reveals deep and hidden things; he knows what lies in dark-*

ness, and light dwells with Him. **I thank and praise you,** *O God of my fathers: You have given me wisdom and power, you have made known to me what we asked of you, you have made known to us the dream of the king."*

You can easily see how Daniel loves the Lord and how he loves to give Him praise. Of course, Daniel has a good reason now, since his life has been spared through this revelation by God to Daniel. However, this prayer goes much deeper. This prayer shows full trust in the God of heaven regardless of the outcome. It shows a deep relationship with the Lord.

Now Daniel is eager to go to the King and tell him about his own dream. Before telling the dream, Daniel makes it very clear to the king that there is only one God in heaven who can reveal mysteries like this. Daniel wants to make sure that God is getting all the praise for this. In verses 31–35 the dream was told. Let us read:

"You looked, O king, and there before you stood a **large statue**—*an enormous, dazzling statue, awesome in appearance. The head of the statue was made of pure gold, its chest and arms of silver, its belly and thighs of bronze, its legs of iron, its feet partly of iron and partly of baked clay. While you were watching,* **a rock** *was cut out, but not by human hands. It* **struck the statue on its feet of iron and clay and smashed them.** *Then the iron, the clay, the bronze, the silver and the gold were broken to pieces at the same time and became like chaff on a threshing floor in the summer. The wind swept them away without leaving a trace. But the rock that struck the statue* **became a huge mountain and filled the whole earth.**"

We can continue to read about the interpretation of the dream in verses 37–45. In the end of verse 38 Daniel says to King Nebuchadnezzar himself: "You are that head of gold." What a spectacular thing. When the king later on realized that his dream covered the whole world history, all the way down to the second coming of Jesus, he must have felt very good about himself, probably more flattered than anyone can handle. Consequently, there is no surprise that King Nebuchadnezzar in Chapter 3 tries to make such an image. His self esteem cannot be higher. In verse 39 we hear about the world empires 2 and 3. Both will be inferior in comparison to Babylon. Then in verse 40 we read:

> *"Finally, there will be a **fourth kingdom, strong as iron**—for iron breaks and smashes everything— and as iron breaks things to pieces, so it will crush and break all the others."*

In other chapters of Daniel, we have already understood that the second world empire was Media— Persia (Daniel 8:20), and the third one was Greece (Daniel 8:21). All these powers will be world powers according to the last part of verse 39. The text above starts with the word "finally." It seems to be both the fourth and the last of the world powers. Everything coming afterwards is only a part of or separate from the fourth kingdom. No more world power will emerge. Several have tried during history to create world empires, like Napoleon, Hitler, Communism, etc., with no success. The old world seems to be impossible to unite. That is further supported by the next verses, 41–43:

> *"Just as you saw that the feet and toes were partly of baked clay and partly of iron, so this **will be a divided kingdom**; yet it will have some strength of iron in it, even as you saw iron mixed with clay. As the toes were partly iron and partly clay, so this kingdom will be **partly strong and partly brittle**. And just as you saw the iron mixed with baked clay, so the **people will be a mixture and will not remain united**, any more than iron mixes with clay."*

Since the Roman Empire is the last of the four kingdoms, the feet and toes must be a part of the same kingdom and area and will never be united into one political power again. If it would happen, then it could only be for a short time, since it says "it will not remain united." That means the European market will never be successfully united for more than, at most, a short time. This is what this vision tells us. It also says that the people will not be united either. The vision also tells us that some countries will be strong and some will not. This is exactly the picture we have today. The countries after the Roman Empire are really fulfilling the prophecy. In the next verses, 44–45, we read:

> *"In the time of those kings, the **God of heaven will set up a kingdom that will never be destroyed**, nor will it be left to another people. It will crush all those kingdoms and bring them to an end, but it will itself **endure forever**. This is the meaning of the vision of the **rock** coming out of a mountain, but not by human hands—a rock that broke the iron, the bronze, the silver and the gold to pieces."*

Since we currently live in the time of the divided feet and toes, it is now time for the rock to come and destroy all the countries. It does not hit the thigh or the legs, etc., but the feet. That means that God will in this age set up his heavenly kingdom, which will last forever. The only time a kingdom is set up is at the second coming of Jesus. When Jesus comes back, all kingdoms will be destroyed, not only the feet but the whole statue, as we read in verse 45. The kingdoms will not only be destroyed, but they will became like chaff and be swept away by the wind without leaving any trace. The threshing floor symbolizes the judgment, which means separation of the wheat from the chaff. If you read John the Baptist's comment about Jesus Christ in Matthew 3:12 you find:

> *"His winnowing fork is in his hand, and he will **clear his threshing floor**, gathering the wheat into the barn and **burning up the chaff** with unquenchable fire."*

At the time of judgment the wheat or the children of

God will be gathered into the barn, and the chaff, or the wicked, will burn up and disappear. God shows here that He has no intention of keeping the wicked alive after the fulfillment of the judgment. There is not a trace left. In verse 35 we read that the rock became a big mountain that filled the whole earth. A mountain is a picture of a kingdom. God's kingdom will take over the whole earth, and nothing but God's kingdom will exist. That means also that there is no room for a hell.[1] The whole earth was filled with God's kingdom. The thing that hit the statue was a rock. In Psalm 19:14 we read:

*"O Lord, my **Rock** and my Redeemer."*

This is another wonderful aspect of this vision. The rock is, in many places in the Bible, the picture of God and especially Jesus Christ. So the rock coming and crushing the statue is Jesus Himself at His second coming. The rock as well as the redeemer is hitting the earth. This is well in harmony with Jesus' parables about His second coming. The rock is destroying the wicked and the redeemer is saving the saints. In the last part of Daniel 2:45, we read:

*"The great God has shown the king what will take place in the future. The dream is **true** and the interpretation is **trustworthy**."*

These words, "true" and "trustworthy," are also attributes of Jesus Christ. For example, when Jesus is giving His revelation about Himself to John, He uses the same words. In Revelation 21:5 and 6 we read:

*"He who was seated on the throne said, 'I am making everything new!' Then he said, 'Write this down, for these words are **trustworthy** and **true**.' He said to me: 'It is done. **I am the Alpha and Omega**, the Beginning and the End. To him who is thirsty I will give to drink without cost from the spring of the water of life.'"*

With this connection to the book of Revelation, we

---

[1] For further study, please read the author's book "The Second Coming of Jesus in a New Perspective."

can recognize Jesus Christ in this prophecy of Daniel as well. When King Nebuchadnezzar heard this, he was utterly amazed and fell prostrate before Daniel and gave him all kinds of honor. He also placed Daniel in a high position and made him ruler over the entire province of Babylon and placed him in charge of all the wise men. Daniel did not forget his three friends, and after Daniel's request they were appointed administrators of the province of Babylon. Surely, Daniel did not forget God in this. It would be a big surprise if Daniel and his friends did not spend a lot of time in giving thanks and praise to the God of heaven. They all had reason to be thankful. We cannot end this vision without receiving the final point about King Nebuchadnezzar. In Daniel 2:47 we read:

> *"The king said to Daniel, 'Surely your God is the God of gods and the Lord of kings and a revealer of mysteries, for you were able to reveal this mystery.'"*

This is a very accurate statement, even if it is coming from an unconverted heart. This is the kind of statement we all will express when we meet God in the judgment. If we only see a small part of God or of Him in action, we will all realize the magnitude of the only living God whether we believe in God or not. He is awesome in all aspects, and the only natural way of expressing this encounter is to worship Him. This is exactly what King Nebuchadnezzar did in this verse.

With this vision, God revealed His plan for the earth, from the current situation with Daniel and his people in captivity in Babylon all the way through history and ending up with the second coming of Jesus and the establishing of the everlasting kingdom. This dream and its fantastic interpretation give us today the basic guidelines for our understanding of the world order. This also shows us the attitude of God. He wants to reveal information to us in the right amount at the right time so we can have confidence in Him and the proper understanding of the time we are living in. According to this vision, the next big event in God's world history will be the second coming of Jesus.

Daniel: Chapter 4

Chapter 4 starts quite differently. There is no real time information, like in many other chapters. Chapters 7–10 all start out with what year of the reigning king we are dealing with, but not here. Something is different. We know that we are studying a dream of King Nebuchadnezzar, who is the king in Babylon. In another way this chapter is also starting differently. We are right away receiving a proclamation. The Bible does not tell if this is part of the vision or not. When starting to read it, we are left in confusion for a while. However, when reading the chapter, you will find the reason for the difference. The first 18 verses are described in "I" form, and it is King Nebuchadnezzar himself who is telling the story. With that in mind, we are ready to see what he wants to say. We must remember that this king, according to Daniel Chapter 2, is probably the most important, mighty and prosperous king ever on this earth. He himself is the golden head, according to the first vision in Chapter 2 of Daniel. Can you imagine? This heathen king has written a part of the Bible. Since God has allowed him to do that, it must be for a good reason. Now we let the king proclaim, and we start in verse 1 and read to verse 3:

> *"King Nebuchadnezzar, To the peoples, nations, and men of every language, who live in all the world: May you prosper greatly! It is my pleasure to tell you about the miraculous signs and wonders that **the Most High God** has performed for me. How great are his signs, how mighty his wonders!* ***His kingdom is an eternal kingdom; his dominion endures from generation to generation."***

What a great start. He is very positive. He gives glory and honor to God in heaven in a wonderful and generous way. King Nebuchadnezzar recognizes that God has the ultimate power. What is even more fascinating is that King

Nebuchadnezzar is giving a message to the whole world. He is addressing this to peoples, nations and men of every language. But here is also another surprise. At this point it is not clear why, but he is actually giving a personal testimony to the world about his faith in God. We have not a clue if King Nebuchadnezzar one day will come to heaven or not, but it looks really promising to start with. After this special introduction and proclamation, he goes on to his dream. We read it in verses 4–7:

> *"I, Nebuchadnezzar, was at home in my palace, contented and prosperous. I had a dream that made me afraid. As I was lying in my bed, the images and visions that passed through my mind terrified me. So I commanded that all the wise men of Babylon be brought before me to interpret the dream for me. When the **magicians, enchanters, astrologers and diviners** came, I told the dream, but **they could not interpret it for me**."*

In Chapter 2, the king did not remember the dream itself. But here it is different. The king knows the dream but does not know what to do with it. He is terrified and he is afraid but has no solution. He senses that something is not good, but he does not know what it means. He is eager to know and starts to act accordingly. He is gathering all the wise men around him. Maybe we would today say that he called in the government and his advisers. The wise men probably remember what happened last time they failed, as we read in Chapter 2. At that time, the king was ready to kill them all. This time the king seems to be in a more harmonic state, and no threats are mentioned. The reason for this is probably the remembrance of Daniel and his connection to the Most High God. Also the king's lesson about the fiery furnace has probably given him an indication of who is in charge. In both these stories, the king learned to know about the almighty God, and these two events are very likely the reason for his testimony above. Let us continue to read verses 8–10:

> *"Finally, Daniel came into my presence and I told*

*him the dream. (He is called Belteshazzar, after the name of my God, and the spirit of the holy gods is in him.) I said, Belteshazzar, chief of the magicians, I know that **the spirit of the holy gods** is in you, and no mystery is too difficult for you. Here is my dream; interpret it for me. These are the visions I saw while lying in my bed."*

Yes, he remembered Daniel very well. The word "finally" probably indicated that the king was waiting for Daniel. All the other wise men came, but no one could help the king. Finally Daniel showed up, the chief of them all, and the king related the story to him, and it seems that the king had a lot of confidence in Daniel. The king still believed in many gods, but the god of Daniel gets the prefix "the holy." Now the king tells us his dream as we read from verses 10–12:

*"I looked and there before me stood a **tree** in the middle of the land. Its **height was enormous**. The tree grew large and strong and its top touched the sky; It was visible to the end of the earth. Its leaves were **beautiful**, its fruit **abundant** and on it was food for all. Under it the beasts of the field found **shelter**, and the birds of the air lived in its branches; from it every creature was fed."*

What a special kingdom! Have you ever heard such a heavenly announcement about the harmony in all the country? There was peace throughout the land. It was enough food for everyone, etc. We do not know enough about the rest of the world powers, but during the Babylonian age and under King Nebuchadnezzar, it seems that there were no hungry or homeless people. Even the cattle, the birds, and all other animals were included. It is almost too hard to believe. And then, of course, we have this big tree. The tree is standing in the middle of the land. The king is the center. All the power is in his hands. Everyone in this kingdom seems to know about him. And even if the tree is so enormously high, in the next sentence it says "it grew." The tree is described as strong and large. The last part of this sentence is interesting. It says that the top touched the sky. Another word for sky could be "heaven." This tree is so enormous that it is approaching heaven. Let us remember this in our further study. In verses 13–17 we can read the rest of the dream:

> *"In the visions I saw while lying in my bed, I looked, and there before me was **a messenger, a holy one, coming down from heaven**. He called in a loud voice: **cut down the tree** and trim off its branches; strip off its leaves and scatter its fruit. Let the animals flee from under it and the birds from its branches. But let the stump and its roots, bound with iron and bronze, remain in the ground in the grass of the field. Let him be drenched with the dew of heaven, and let him live with the animals among the plants of the earth. Let his mind be changed from that of a man and let him be given the mind of an animal, **till seven times pass by for him**. The decision is announced by messengers, the holy ones declare the verdict, **so that the living may know that the Most High is sovereign over the kingdoms of men and gives them to anyone he wishes** and sets over them the lowliest of men."*

What a dream! In one way or another, the king realizes that this is an intervention from God. We have words like "messenger," "holy one," and "heaven." So the king has no doubt about the source. Maybe that is the reason for the initial proclamation. He seems to know who is in charge. Is this knowledge a reality from the bottom of his heart or not? In the dream itself, there is actually so much information already given that we can get the feeling that the king pretty much understood the message. It is a verdict. Maybe he wished to hear that the verdict is for someone else. Already here, when the tree has been cut off, the text says "him" and not the word "tree." The verdict is meant to show that the Most High is sovereign over the kingdoms and kings. If this was the reason for the vision in that day, what about today? In that day, this point was very important to God. If God does not change, which we read in Malachi 3:6, is this fact still the truth today? Is God in charge?

THE INTERPRETATION...

In verse 18 the king clearly shows his confidence in Daniel and expects to get an answer. The reason is that the Spirit of the Holy One lives in Daniel. The king knows this. Up till here, the king has been writing the story. But now there is a change. From now on Daniel is stepping in, and the rest of the chapter is seen from Daniel's eyes, except verses 34–37, where the king again is the writer. At first Daniel is perplexed. He is not saying anything. Maybe Daniel is somewhat afraid. If he tells the truth, which is very bad news for the king, what will then happen? Possibly Daniel is scared for his life. The king can see his reaction and encourages Daniel to tell the interpretation. Even after that opening from the king, Daniel is very diplomatic. Before he tells the story, he wishes that the verdict is for the king's enemies. Finally he has to be clear in his statement. In verses 22–23 we read:

> *"**You, O king, are that tree!** You have become great and strong; your greatness has grown until it reaches the sky, and your dominion extends to distant parts of the earth. You, O king, saw a messenger, a holy one, coming down from heaven and saying, '**cut down the tree** and destroy it, but leave the stump, bound with iron and bronze, in the grass of the field, while its roots remain in the ground. Let him be drenched with the dew of heaven; let him live like the animals, until seven times pass by for him.'"*

In Strong's concordance, the word times is called a "technical term." There it says that a "time" is the same as a year. Seven times is then consequently seven years. Daniel continues to explain the dream for the king. Nebuchadnezzar will lose his sanity and be driven out to live like an animal. But why all this? What is the reason for it? Didn't we say that he started out quite good? In verse

25 God is telling the king, through the voice of Daniel, why:

> *"Seven times will pass by for you **until you ac-knowledge** that the Most High is sovereign over the kingdoms of men and gives them to anyone he wishes."*

At this point, it does not seem adequate to talk about pride and selfishness. Actually, the king has so far shown more honor to the living God than most rulers do today. Are the words of Nebuchadnezzar true or not? Is Nebuchadnezzar talking without standing behind the real meaning? Is this a prophecy? Can we influence the prophecy? Daniel actually tries to do that in the last part of his explanation. With this he wants to give the king a chance to prevent something bad from coming. In verse 27 we read:

> *"Therefore, O king, be pleased to accept my advice: **Renounce your sins** by doing what is right, and your wickedness by being kind to the oppressed. **It may be that then your prosperity will continue."***

We can draw several lessons from this. We have this prophecy in Chapter 4 of Daniel, and God has given it to us to draw the right conclusion from it. One is that God warns enough that no one can blame God for anything. With this story, we have to learn that God is in charge. Even today, God is following the destinies in this world. Jesus supported this by saying that the very hairs on our heads are counted. And not a bird is falling to the ground without that the heavenly Father knows about it. When you have studied the gospels and the love of Jesus, when you know that this love of Jesus is one with the Father in heaven, is this event for the king a punishment or an action in love? Is this action there to prevent the king from being lost eternally? We have all the right to form our lives as we like. God did not stop the king. But God can foresee events and He can also look into our hearts. Because of that, He can help those whom He loves. Of course, this is said in an eternal perspective, but as often as possible God also tries in an earthly perspective to help us. This act of God to "cut off the tree" is an act of love. Let us see why.

THE DREAM FULFILLED...

The upcoming event will tell us the reason for this story. God knows what will happen in the future. He is willing to send messengers to warn the person. He even gives advice, through Daniel, how to escape the ominous proclaimed future. God gives us a way out of our dilemma. And if we go back, we find that God tried with many events to draw the king's attention to the Most High. God gave him a plan to follow. He announced it very clearly. Why did not the king follow? Because the king has a free will, just as you and I have a free will. We can choose whom we want to follow. This free will is given to us from God from the time of His creation of this world. In spite of this acting of God towards the king, the king had sovereignty about his own will. Now we will see what is happening. Let us read from verses 28–33:

> "*All this happened to King Nebuchadnezzar. Twelve months later, as the king was walking on the roof of the royal palace of Babylon, he said, 'Is not this the great Babylon **I have** built as the royal residence, by **my mighty power** and for the glory of **my majesty**?' The words were still on his lips when a voice came from heaven, 'This is what is decreed for you, King Nebuchadnezzar: Your royal authority has been taken from you. You will be driven away from people and will live with the wild animals; you will eat grass like cattle. Seven times will pass by for you **until you acknowledge that the Most High is sovereign over the kingdoms of men and gives them to anyone he wishes**.' Immediately what had been said about Nebuchadnezzar was fulfilled.'*"

King Nebuchadnezzar had not learned the lesson. In

spite of the warnings and the events before, he still was too proud. He gave himself the honor and not God. We have earlier seen that there were times when he did recognize the Most High as the sovereign power over the kingdoms of the earth. But this knowledge and recognition of God was not strong enough in his mind to stay there for the future. When he saw all the things around him, his palace, etc., he gave himself the glory. The king thought and said that he was the one who was in charge. He forgot God and God's part in the history of mankind. He lifted up himself instead of giving honor and thanks to God. At that moment the conditions for the prophecy were fulfilled, and then the consequences of the prophecy had to take place. God has not changed. He waited for the fulfillment and acted according to His plan. There was no delay. God acted immediately. Nebuchadnezzar was driven away from people and lived like a wild animal for seven years. Now the question is, what will happen next? In verses 34–35 we read:

> "*At the end of that time, I Nebuchadnezzar, raised my eyes toward heaven, and my sanity was restored. Then **I praised the Most High: I honored and glorified him who lives forever**. His dominion is an eternal dominion; his kingdom endures from generation to generation. All the peoples of the earth are regarded as nothing. He does as he pleases with the powers of heaven and the peoples of the earth. No one can hold back his hand or say to him: 'What have you done?'*"

Not before and not after, but at the right time, the king changed his mind. Why, do you say? Since this was a punishment or a teaching lesson from God, God made sure it came to pass. God has two strong characters. One is His tremendous love that no one can change and which is so much more and so much deeper than we ever will be able to understand. The other is His justice, which is absolute. These two things might seem to be in contradiction to each other, especially for us human beings. But for God, who knows the end from the beginning, this is not a problem.

He can balance these two components in a wonderful and blessed way. We can either trust him or not believe him, that He is capable. We as human beings are trained to question things with the background that I can do it better or change situations to something more efficient. That is all correct when we are dealing with humans. But when we are dealing with the Most High, we have to look with another perspective. King Nebuchadnezzar even said, after going through this humbling experience, that no one can question Him or say to Him, "What have you done, O, Lord." If we understand God, there is no room for this question. The question is not adequate. It is not appropriate. If you do not agree, you are strongly encouraged to give yourself fully to Him and let Him, through the word and the spirit, in prayer and Bible study, show you what He deems best. In the last two verses of this Chapter 4, we find the converted King Nebuchadnezzar. In verses 36–37 we read:

> *"At the same time that my sanity was restored, my honor and splendor were returned to me for the glory of my kingdom. My advisers and nobles sought me out, and **I was restored to my throne and became even greater than before.** Now I, Nebuchadnezzar, **praise and exalt and glorify the King of heaven,** because **everything he does is right** and **all his ways are just.** And those who walk in pride he is able to humble."*

The faith and trust the king is showing towards the God of heaven is greater than many Christians seem to have. If this is the case, we will surely meet King Nebuchadnezzar in heaven. We should learn from this heathen king to give glory, honor and praise to our God, regardless of the circumstances. The king learned the lesson; have we? Let us read from Proverbs Chapter 3:5–6:

> *"Trust in the Lord with **all your heart** and lean **not** on your own understanding; in all your ways acknowledge him, and he will make your paths straight."*

Isn't this the message of this vision? Trust your God in all circumstances. He is able and full of love. He has a wonderful plan for you, even if you do not see it right now. In this plan He gives you a free choice all the time. He warns you because of His love for you. He has a way out of the problems. Maybe not as you think, but trust Him! A prophecy is not a predetermination of things but a wonderful plan from a foreseeing God. Later on no one can come and accuse God. He has done everything He possibly can to give you the best, according to His tremendous love.

Daniel: Chapter 7

This is the third vision in the book of Daniel. This vision is given to Daniel as well as the explanation. The vision does not have a specific address and seems to be dealing with the world order, similar to vision number one. The first vision ended with God's everlasting kingdom making an end to all other kingdoms. This third vision is dealing with how the situation will be at the day of judgment. In the first verse of Chapter 7, we know that we are in historic time and, to be more exact, in the first year of Belshazzar, King of Babylon. Daniel had a dream, which he writes down. In verse 2–3 we read:

> "Daniel said; 'In my vision at night I looked, and there before me were the four winds of heaven churning up the great sea. **Four great beasts**, each different from the others, came up out of the sea.'"

It seems obvious that the start is similar to vision number one. We are here dealing with four beasts of four kingdoms. They are all great and represent world power. They are all different from each other, telling us that they are not only four kings in the same kingdom but really four very different empires. They are stirred up by the four winds of heaven, indicating that they are all coming on stage according to the plan of a wonderful God. Coming out of the sea usually represents coming out of the existing people. It is not a new people coming from outside of the world but from present populations. In verse 4 we continue to read:

> "The first was like a **lion**, and it had the wings of an eagle. I watched until its wings were torn off and it was lifted from the ground so that it stood on two feet like a man, and the heart of a man was given to it."

Those who are well versed in history know that the lion was the symbol Babylon used to represent its own kingdom. The four animal kingdoms are very similar to the four world powers described in Daniel Chapters 2, 8 and 11. When reading Chapter 2:37, we know that the first world power was meant to be Babylon. We also know from previous chapters that King Nebuchadnezzar was the first and the greatest king of Babylon. He became too boastful and was in a dream shown how he, as a big tree, was cut down. We can read this story in Chapter 4. The reason for this was his lack of humility towards God in heaven. For seven years he had to live as an animal until he realized that "the Most High is sovereign over the kingdoms of men and gives them to anyone He wishes." In Chapter 4:34 we read:

> "At the end of that time, **I Nebuchadnezzar,** raised my eyes toward heaven, and my sanity was restored. Then I praised the Most High; **I honored and glorified Him** who lives forever. His dominion is an eternal dominion..."

After being very proud of himself, King Nebuchadnezzar became humble before God. This raised him up from the level of an animal and he stood on two legs. He became humane. This is also reinforced by giving him a heart of a man. It is meant to be a "heart of a man" in God's eyes. This picture fits very well with King Nebuchadnezzar and, with him, the empire by name of Babylon. In verses 5–6 of Chapter 7 we read:

> "And there before me was a second beast, which looked like a **bear**. It was raised up on one of its sides, and it had three ribs in its mouth between its teeth. It was told, 'Get up and eat your fill of flesh!' After that, I looked, and there before me was another beast, one that looked like a **leopard**. And on its back it had four wings like those of a bird. This beast had four heads, and it was given authority to rule."

Since many books have been written about the identification of these beasts, we can quickly accept the Bible's own explanation for these two world powers. In Daniel

8:20 we read about Media and Persia being world power number two, and in verse 21 we read about empire number three being Greece. For the historical scholar, there are many more details of encouragement in these pictures to be found. As we have seen so far, the world history is passing very quickly before our eyes, only one verse per world power. Obviously this is not the focus of the vision. In verse 7 we read about the fourth beast:

> *"After that, in my vision at night I looked, and there before me was a **fourth beast**—terrifying and frightening and very powerful. It had large iron teeth; it crushed and devoured its victims and trampled underfoot whatever was left. It was different from all the former beasts, and it had **ten horns.**"*

The fourth great kingdom is considered to be the Roman Empire. It is here described as something very powerful and frightening, and iron seems to be the best symbol. In the vision about the statue, the legs were also made of iron and given the same character as in this chapter. Hardly anything can match the systematic power and cruelty of the Roman Empire. In the last part of this verse we read about its 10 horns. In the first vision the Roman Empire was followed by the 10 toes. These 10 horns or toes are often considered to be 10 European states which were coming up after the fall of the Roman Empire. But again, only one verse is given to the Roman Empire and the European states. And even more surprisingly, the explanation for these four powers by the angel is done in one verse. In verse 17 we read:

> *"The four great beasts are four kingdoms that will rise from the earth."*

So what is the point? The sentence is very short and concise. It is obviously not the order of the four beasts or what they represent which is important. The four kingdoms are only setting the stage for what is yet to come out of this vision. The 10 horns are very quickly explained in verse 24:

> *"The ten horns are ten kings who will come from this kingdom."*

It does not seem that the ten horns are the center of this vision either. We also saw that the 10 horns are subsequently emerging from the Roman Empire. The outcome of this vision could, however, be considered in verse 18:

> *"But the saints of the Most High will receive the kingdom and will possess it forever—yes, for ever and ever."*

This is the goal with this vision, to show the winning side. The four earthly kingdoms are here contrasted to the heavenly kingdom. The four described kingdoms last for a short time, compared to the heavenly kingdom, which will last forever and ever. But how is it possible to come from the earthly kingdoms to the heavenly kingdom? There must be some events in between. In the first vision in Daniel Chapter 2, we went from the ten toes directly to the heavenly kingdom. In Chapter 7 we see many verses describing this in between. Maybe this "in between" is the message in this vision. Before we study this, let us continue up till the central part of this chapter. The vision goes on and in verse 8 we read:

> *"While I was thinking about the horns, there before me was **another horn, a little one**, which came up among them; and three of the first horns were uprooted before it. This horn had eyes like eyes of a man and a mouth that spoke boastfully."*

What is the meaning of this horn? This little horn has more space in this chapter then the other world powers. Besides, in verse 8, quoted above, we can also read one and a half verses of explanation from the angel. To get the whole picture of the little horn, we have to read from the last part of verse 24 and verse 25:

> *"After them (10 horns) **another king** will arise, **different** from the earlier ones; he will subdue three kings. He will **speak against the Most High** and*

*oppress His saints and try to **change the set times
and laws**. The saints will be handed over for a
time, times and half a time."*

The little horn is coming to power after the ten European states were formed, since he comes after the 10
horns. This little horn must be powerful, since he had
power to uproot three other horns. These three horns were
once three of the initial ten horns. This little horn cannot
be the Roman Empire, since that has already disappeared
and given way for the ten horns. The horn should also be
different compared to the other 10 horns. These 10 horns
are political powers, but this one should not be. There is
only one power that meets all these criteria; that is the
Papacy. The Papacy is a religious power and not a political power. It was behind the extinction of the Ostrogoths,
the Vandals and the Visigoths. The papacy has been a per-
secuting power. It has also tried to change the set times
and the laws. The Papacy is still today taking the responsibility for changing the worshipping on the seventh day
of the week to the first day of the week. This is an attack on
the Ten Commandments, which still is the law of God.
This is the only commandment dealing with holy time.
Since holy time is instituted by God and not by men, any
attempt to change the "set times and laws" is a rebellion
against God. This is one way of blaspheming against God.
The Catholic Church has made several claims over the
years to be responsible for this change of "set times and
laws." Please read the following Catholic statements.

"In response to the question, 'Have you any other
way of proving that the church has power to in-
stitute festivals of precept?' Stephen Keenan
wrote, 'Had she not such power, she could not
have done that in which all modern religionists
agree with her—she could not have substituted
the observance of Sunday, the first day of the
week, for the observance of Saturday, the seventh day, a change for which there is no Scrip-
tural authority'" —Stephen Keenan, A Doctrinal
Catechism, p. 174.

"You may read the Bible from Genesis to Revelation and you will not find a single line authorizing the sanctification of Sunday. The scripture enforces the religious observance of Saturday, a day which we never sanctify" —Cardinal Gibbons, Faith of Our Fathers, p. 111, 112.

In this world, we are either for or against God. There is nothing in between, or better said: What is in between is against God. Jesus says in Matthew 12:30 "He who is not with me is against me." That means we are either on the devil's side or on God's side. This could be a long-term situation but also a short-term issue. When we look at the life of Peter, we have quotations from him coming from both sides. In Mark 8:33 we read:

"But when Jesus turned and looked at his disciples, He rebuked Peter. 'Get behind me Satan!' He said. 'You do not have in mind the things of God, but the things of men.'"

You do not have in mind the things of God but maybe your own thought, maybe your own perception, understanding, etc. We will all be responsible for that and ask for forgiveness. But if we persist in this fashion, it can be a matter of rebellion towards God. The devil is in all these circumstances. Ultimately Satan is responsible for all resistance and rebellion towards God. That is why we, in Revelation 13, meet both the "horn" and the dragon in verses 3–4. In Revelation 13 the horn is called "the beast." Let us read from verses 4–8:

"**Men worshipped the dragon** because he had given authority to the beast, **and they also worshipped the beast** and asked, 'Who is like the beast? Who can make war against him? The beast was given a mouth to utter **proud words** and blasphemies and to exercise his authority for **forty-two months**. He opened his mouth to **blaspheme God**, and to **slander his name** and his dwelling place and those who live in heaven. He was given power to **make war against the saints** and to conquer them. And

> *he was given authority over every tribe, people, lan-*
> *guage and nation. All inhabitants of the earth will*
> *worship the beast—all whose names have not been*
> *written in the book of life belonging to the Lamb*
> *that was slain from the creation of the world.'"*

In Revelation the beast was given authority for 42 months to make war against the saints. This time is the same as 1,260 days or 3 and a half prophetic years. In Daniel 7:25 we read that the "saints will be handed over to him (the little horn) for a time, times and half a time." This time period means one year, two years and half a year. That is the same as three and a half years or 1,260 days or 42 months. With that time in mind, you can see all the similarities between the little horn in Daniel 7 and the beast in Revelation 13. In Revelation we read that they worshipped both the beast and the dragon because the dragon had given the authority to the beast. The point here is that the dragon or Satan is behind all this and ultimately he is responsible for all rebellion. Regardless of the name of a religion, denomination, group or person, to be against God comes always from the devil. Simon Peter was used by the devil in our example above from Mark 8:33. In spite of that, Jesus Christ continued to love Peter with all His heart. We should always have Jesus Christ as our example. We also ought to love any person regardless of his or her attitude or belief. Think about Jesus on the cross or at the stoning of Stephen. Both prayed for their persecutors. Our God is the only one who eventually will and can judge. He alone knows about each person acting in a persecution. God alone knows the heart of the persecutors and knows if one person just faithfully followed an order without having full understanding or if a person was filled by the devil and doing a mean act. But please, do not mix religious politics with Jesus' command to "love your neighbor as yourself." After the little horn had been speaking and acting boastfully, Daniel continued to look as the vision went on. Let us read from the first of verse 9:

> "As I looked, **thrones** were set in place, and the
> **Ancient of Days took His seat.**"

The Ancient of Days is then described with almost two verses. His clothing was white as snow and His hair was white like wool. His throne was flaming with fire and a river of fire was coming out from before Him. It also mentions how many were serving and acting around Him. Thousands upon thousands attended Him and ten thousands upon ten thousands stood before Him. This description must be of God, the Father Himself. What a majestic picture! After the description of God the Father and in the end of verse 10 we read:

> *"The **court** was **seated** and the **books were opened**."*

In the first text above we find out who the court is. It is the Father of the universe because the only one who took his seat was the Father. To be seated also means to go into action or to start the judging process. That is again indicated in the phrase about the books. They are opened and the procedure can begin. In verse 26 and 27 we again find a good connection to the two texts above.

> *"But the **court will sit**, and his power will be taken away and completely destroyed forever. **Then the sovereignty, power and greatness** of the kingdoms under the whole heaven **will be handed over to the saints**, the people of the Most High. His kingdom will be an **everlasting kingdom**, and all rulers will worship and obey Him."*

When this court is sitting and passing the judgment, it does not seem to be about human individuals here. Of course the group called saints is defined. However, how this group of saints is determined is not the issue here. The turning over of the power from somebody or something to somebody else seems to be the message. Before this process, the world has not been under "the saints." It will, however, eventually be turned over to them. If we now read verse 21, the whole picture will be more clear, especially about the ruler:

> *"As I watched, this **horn** was waging **war against***

the saints and defeating them, until the Ancient of Days came and pronounced judgment in favor of the saints of the Most High, and the time came when they possessed the kingdom."

First we can see that the enemy of the saints is the horn. In verse 8 it is described as the "little horn." This horn will be under judgment and the power of the world will be handed over to the saints. We have already studied who this little horn is and what this power does represent. We need to establish the time for this event. For that question, we read verses 13 and 14:

*"In my vision at night I looked, and there before me was one like a **Son of Man, coming with the clouds of heaven**. He approached the Ancient of Days and was led into His presence. **He was given authority, glory and sovereign power**; all peoples, nations and men of every language worshipped Him. His dominion is an **everlasting dominion** that will not pass away, and **his kingdom is one that will never be destroyed**."*

Here we can understand the timing. This is happening when the Son of Man is coming with the clouds of heaven. This must be the second coming of Jesus. When else is the Son of Man coming on the clouds of heaven? The saints will also be there, since they are the ones who will receive the kingdom after the pronounced judgment. Even if the saints are the recipients of the kingdom, the real victory belongs to Jesus Christ. He is the one who won the victory. It was the blood of the Lamb in Revelation 12 who successfully threw the devil and his angels out of heaven. This victory was accomplished at the cross. Now at the time of the end, at the second coming of Jesus, the consequences of this victory will be visible, not only for the saints, but for everyone in the universe. Jesus Christ receives here all his attributes as a victorious king. He receives authority, glory and sovereign power. And even more, every person in this world is worshipping Christ. Not one is excluded according to the text above. The sentence of the judge is also irrevocable. The new kingdom will never end and never be destroyed. It will last forever. The consequence of the judgment in Daniel 7:11 is that finally the beast was slain. In verse 11 we read:

> "Then I continued to watch because of the boastful words the horn was speaking. **I kept looking until the beast was slain** and its body destroyed and thrown into the blazing fire."

It actually does not precisely say when the beast was slain. Daniel says that he kept looking until the beast was slain. Since the judgment started after the coming of the Son of Man with the clouds and after the judgment of the Ancient of Days and the giving of the authority over to Jesus and His saints, the destroying of the horn or the beast probably is in one of the plagues. It is, by the way, interesting to find in the verse we read above the word "horn" in the first sentence and the word "beast" in the second. This really shows how interchangeable these two words are.

With this Chapter 7 we have now seen the importance of this vision. God is here emphasizing the change of world order at the time of His second coming. The wicked will eventually be destroyed, but the saints will be victorious due to the victory of Jesus Christ on the cross. Here we can see the implementation of His death on the cross. If Jesus had failed, the wicked would not have been destroyed and the saints would never have been rewarded. The consequences of the cross also have importance for the whole universe. If sin eventually is not destroyed, the last quotation from Daniel 7:27 could not be fulfilled:

> "Then the sovereignty, power and greatness of the kingdoms **under the whole heaven** will be handed over to the saints, the people of the Most High."

This indicates that the whole universe was involved in the judgment and not only this earth. This judgment is the cleaning process of everything existing in this universe which is sinful. Any being in the whole universe who has seen the first part of the world's history must also see the final part of it. Every being must be 100% content with the final judgment. There cannot be room for any doubt in anyone's mind in regard to God's justice. God has to prove Himself to be righteous and at the same time full of grace. When this is achieved in the final judgment in this world's history, the whole universe is cleansed. Every living being will thereafter trust Him fully.

In verse 28 we read: "This is the end of the matter." This is fulfilled in many ways: The end of the vision, the end of the explanation and the end of the age. God has finally shown complete and everlasting justice.